Song Offerings

GITANJALI

RABINDRANATH TAGORE

Song Offerings

(GITANJALI)

TRANSLATED AND INTRODUCED BY

JOE WINTER

ANVIL PRESS POETRY

Published in 2000
by Anvil Press Poetry Ltd
Neptune House   70 Royal Hill   London SE10 8RF
Originally published in 1998 by P. Lal
WRITERS WORKSHOP, Calcutta

This book is published
with financial assistance from
The Arts Council of England

Set in Monotype Fournier by Anvil
Printed and bound in England
by Cromwell Press, Trowbridge, Wiltshire

ISBN 0 85646 311 6

Cover photograph: Rabindranath Tagore at Santiniketan
at the time of writing *Gitanjali*

A catalogue record for this book
is available from the British Library

I give back to you the echo of your song

RABINDRANATH TAGORE

I am grateful to the many friends who have given themselves heart and mind to the task whenever asked.

J.W.

To Gauri Ayyub of Calcutta

Introduction

FOR THOSE WHO speak Bengali, the inhabitants of West Bengal and Bangladesh (and the world-wide Bengali diaspora), Rabindranath Tagore is virtually a breathing presence. Some may not know many of his words yet are conscious of him in the way that India at large may be said to be conscious of Gandhi – that is, conscious *with* him. His songs and poetry are only part of what he gave, his life itself was a monument of giving, the man of vision and the man of action working to the limits of the individual to celebrate existence. For him this also meant working for a better world. One wonders whether the visionary and the man of outward action, the maker of dreams and the taker of initiatives, could exist side by side in the same person to any deeper or broader extent; it seems impossible. The details of his life are remarkable enough; but here it is not the life but one book of his poems that is presented.

Gitanjali is deeply treasured by his people. The title means 'Song-Offerings' in a holy sense. Of the great majority of the poems (it appears not all) the poet made songs. He also re-wrote some of the poems in English, in very different style as will be seen, into prose-poetry; and for a time the English *Gitanjali* was celebrated in the West. Yet while a fine work of literature in its own right, it should be said that in re-presenting the original it also hid it: that what Bengalis know and love is something other. It is time the original work was given more of a chance in the outside world.

The version herein is a rendering of the text as it appears on the Bengali page, 157 poems each musically, intellectually and spiritually of a piece. At least this has been my aim. The whole can be taken too as a single long poem, rhapsodic in mood and structure, a vehicle for an inner journey, the utterance of a soul awake to the beauty of life and life's end.

RABINDRANATH (poets in this part of the world who become 'part of the family' are often referred to by their first name) was born in Calcutta in 1861 and died there in 1941, though I doubt he would have called himself a Calcuttan, being more at home in the open Bengal countryside. Rather than detail his life I seek to present the minimum of biographical information, and let the poems speak for themselves. For those who would know more I recommend four works. First, Krishna Kripalani's *Tagore: a Biography* (Oxford University Press, London and Grove Press, New York, 1962). Kripalani knew Tagore well, worked with him (and married into the family), and wrote with warmth and understanding: one trusts the voice as one reads. He provides a remarkably fine all-round picture. A later biography, at a further remove from the person yet written perhaps a little more in the spirit of enquiry, is *Rabindranath Tagore: the Myriad-Minded Man* by Krishna Dutta and Andrew Robinson (Bloomsbury, 1995). Its marshalling of fact surrounding such a densely-packed life is admirable; and its selection of quotations from Rabindranath's prose is particularly telling. Ketaki Kushari Dyson's introduction to *I Won't Let You Go* (Bloodaxe, 1992) is an excellent encapsulation of Rabindranath in context. In this book she has translated a variety of his poems and songs, including two of the *Gitanjali*. The other well-known translation into English of the poetry is by William Radice, *Rabindranath Tagore: Selected Poems* (Penguin Books, 1985), whose introduction imaginatively proceeds by means of an Upanishadic verse. Applied in stages to the life it allows something to be caught of the character, of the spirit moving him in relation to his writing;

though one or two of the points made are debatable if taken on their own. It is for its approach that I recommend it; and the Notes at the end of the volume are scholarly and clear.

TAGORE WROTE *Gitanjali* from 1906–10 but mostly in the last three months of that period. He dated all the poems after the first few and published them in chronological order of composition. (Readers may like to know that 80, 81 and 82 were written on the same day; as were 112, 113 and 114. Indeed the last three were followed all on the next day by 115, 116, 117 and 118. Also in one day, during which he took a train journey of a few hours, were composed 150, 151, 152, 153, 154 and 155. The labouring translator's bewilderment may be imagined.) It is possible to look at events in his life and see a reflection of a kind in the poems. His awareness of death must have been heightened by the passing-away of his wife and two of his children between 1902 and 1907; as by the earlier death in 1884 of his sister-in-law Kadambari to whom he had a very deep attachment. One might also draw attention to a brief period of active political protest, following Lord Curzon's announcement of the partition of Bengal in 1905, from which he appears to have withdrawn in disillusionment at the way he was being used. But in general one may say they are not the kind of poems to be associated with particular events.

Nor too closely with a particular creed. 'Can you squeeze me behind any one religious boundary?' wrote the poet to a friend and follower, Kalidas Nag. Tagore was a member of the Brahmo Samaj, a breakaway movement from traditional Hinduism, that did not permit idolatry, advocated not detachment from earthly affairs but involvement as the way to salvation, and promoted tolerance for other faiths. It had developed from the pioneering work of Rammohan Roy, a forthright intellectual and social activist of the early nineteenth century. Tagore's father took over and largely organised the movement, weaving together as its backcloth a tapestry taken from the Upanishads, ancient sacred texts that can be described as explorations of the formless divine. With this blend of old and new as a base, so to speak, Rabindranath had a world-wide outlook, admiring especially Christianity and Buddhism. The thrust of his life was at once religious and humanist and so it may be said of these poems, that resist dogmatic interpretation and speak, perhaps, of the 'I' in all. This is at one and the same time universal and Indian poetry. The Upanishads may be said to have found a voice here; and reference to all-powerful figures of Hindu belief is made if not by name. Nature is present in her abundance in storms and clouds, wind and trees and flowers; and no less so, though less named, in her gods.

The poems often treat of earthly and divine love in a marvellous ambiguity as one. A sense of erotic spirituality stemming from the love-play of Krishna and Radha is the tradition behind this, manifesting itself variously in Indian culture and sometimes misunderstood by the West. In *Gitanjali* at times a yearning is expressed in a sense of the formed and the formless at once; and do we not feel the yearning the more?

TAGORE TRANSLATED a number of the *Gitanjali* into English in 1912, at first while recovering from illness and without the energy, as he put it, 'to sit down and write anything new'. He continued the exercise on a voyage to England that year, his first serious venture into English translation, and arrived with a manuscript made up half of *Gitanjali* re-creations and half of pieces from nine other of his books. (He wrote over fifty volumes of poetry in all.) Some material translated was in fact new. The exotic figure, as he must have seemed, with his haunting, prayerful and strangely authoritative offerings, was at once taken up. W. B. Yeats read from the manuscript to a distinguished gathering held in a private London house in Tagore's honour; and it appears Yeats was of some assistance in the selection of finished pieces for the final English text. A little misleadingly, this was given the title of the main contributory volume. The English *Gitanjali* was first published in 1913 and Yeats supplied the introduction, a powerful personal statement amounting almost to a confession, of the magic spun by the poems, the inner light woken in him. The magic worked apace: Tagore left for India in September 1913, after a little over a year in the West; and news of his award of the Nobel Prize for Literature reached him in Santiniketan near Calcutta that November.

The prize may fairly be said to have been awarded for a work of Indian literature in English. (Other self-translation was submitted with *Gitanjali* but that book was the rage.) One member of the Swedish Academy had learnt some Bengali and would have explored the original to some degree. Others read a Swedish translation of the English as well as the English. But it was the English that dominated then, and has dominated since in that virtually all translations including into other Indian languages are from that and not the Bengali original. The reason for that of course was and is the widespread knowledge of English. The original is far and away the finer work. But Tagore's English version does possess a strong identity of its own. Any good translation is also a new work in a different language. Sometimes the departures are such that it is more a new work and less a translation.

The Authorised Version of the Bible, and Fitzgerald's *Rubaiyat of Omar Khayyam*, are perhaps the two outstanding examples in English of literary translation that leaps into a new life, partly by means of a decisive departure from the old. Tagore's self-translation of the *Gitanjali* is a third. In it, instinctively aware of what he could and could not do in English, he gave up the lyric's song-cadence and fashioned a poetic prose. He shortened many pieces; what mattered to him was the jewel's sparkle and to keep that he would cut down on size; and here and there too he changed the sense to fit his new purpose. In English he was able to present a sequence, it might be said, of prayer-lamps; virtually every piece is a single story-picture, briefly shining; and together they present something of a hypnotic effect. Singly they stand out much less than do the originals, with a few exceptions; and the overall effect of the originals is far more than that of a line of prayer-lamps; but rather a deeply-illuminated festival of love. They are prayers and celebrations too, carrying as all true poetry does the hidden recapitulation of music, with any number of verbal glories on the way. Yet the English has its own quieter music. Rather than anticipate the poems' presence with quotation from Tagore's re-working of original *Gitanjali*, I give a piece he took from another volume. (A list of his own translations of *Gitanjali* is appended to the Notes herein.) One of the most memorable pieces of the English collection is from a volume called *Shishu* (Child).

'On the seashore of endless worlds children meet. The infinite sky is motionless overhead and the restless water is boisterous. On the seashore of endless worlds the children meet with shouts and dances.

They build their houses with sand and they play with empty shells. With withered leaves they weave their boats and smilingly float them on the vast deep. Children have their play on the seashore of worlds.

They know not how to swim, they know not how to cast nets. Pearl fishers dive for pearls, merchants sail in their ships, while children gather pebbles and scatter them again. They seek not for hidden treasures, they know not how to cast nets.

The sea surges up with laughter and pale gleams the smile of the sea beach. Death-dealing waves sing meaningless ballads to the children, even like a mother while rocking her baby's cradle. The sea plays with children, and pale gleams the smile of the sea beach.

On the seashore of endless worlds children meet. Tempest roams in the pathless sky, ships get wrecked in the trackless water, death is abroad and children play. On the seashore of endless worlds is the great meeting of children.'

Of the 103 prose-poems of the English *Gitanjali* fifty, of which this is one, are from other books. One feels Tagore might have found a new name for the English volume. The fifty-three that justify the title, as it were, represent only a third of the Bengali

Gitanjali, or rather less as he truncated so many. In the English the order is not chronological. The chief difference however is in the sharp sense of the individual that the original carries; its joy, its immediacy; its keener and fuller exploration of the self as spirit; and overwhelmingly in the quality of the poetry.

THE ORIGINAL *Gitanjali* poems were written first as they appear and have always appeared on the book's pages: unadorned poems. Tagore turned them into songs as or shortly after he wrote; soon these were written down too with their melody (by someone he would sing them to, often a gifted great-nephew). It is as songs that they are known far and wide by Bengali-speakers; yet the text still has a spoken voice. Many appreciate the pieces unsung, whether or not they know the melody for the particular one they are reading. Each poem has a spoken voice to be heard; and some that alone in part or whole. Some verses of a few longer pieces were not used in the song-text; and some complete poems are not and seem never to have been sung.

One cannot overlook Tagore's power and popularity as a song-writer. Bengal (if in this matter one may refer to West Bengal and Bangladesh as the one area of his lifetime) is inheritor to his more than two thousand songs: a living legacy. Famous in his lifetime as a poet, short-story writer, novelist, playwright, essayist, known throughout the world for his lecture tours and in later life as an artist, ceaselessly involved in practical work in the cause of national and international development, it was as a song-writer that he stood surest on the ground of his giving. 'With my songs I have touched the feet of God', once said this diffident man.

But the poems are of importance regardless of their status as songs. It is worth mentioning that the *Gitanjali* songs are not published on their own but in a great collection of Rabindranath's songs; the *Gitanjali* publication as such has always been the poetic text, different overall from that of the songs and without musical notation. Some feel the *Gitanjali* can not really be translated as they are songs and a song needs its melody. William Radice in his *Selected Poems* leaves them alone for this reason. Perhaps now they are translated without further melody than the one the page breathes, as it were, they may in general be allowed their first identity, to accompany the second. And the poems that are not known as songs may perhaps be recognised more and seen to have their place in the whole. There is in fact a distinction of meaning between poem and song though they may use the same words. The intellectual drive that can exist low-key in lyric poetry is noticeable in a good many of the following pieces; while in the songs it naturally falls away to some extent though never absent. The songs' melody is of course much greater. If the spoken songs, then, may have their melody too, one hopes the beauty of the originals may come more to view; and that the songs that are sung will attract a wider audience in their turn.

IN 1921 TAGORE went to Stockholm and gave his acceptance speech for the Nobel Prize of eight years before. In this extract we glimpse the writing of *Gitanjali* in the context of his life as well as his immediate surroundings.

'I remember how my life's work developed from the time when I was very young. When I was about 25 years I used to live in utmost seclusion in the solitude of an obscure Bengal village by the river Ganges in a boat-house. The wild ducks which came during the time of autumn from the Himalayan lakes were my only living companions, and in that solitude I seem to have drunk in the open space like wine overflowing with sunshine, and the murmur of the river used to speak to me and tell me the secrets of nature. And I passed my days in the solitude dreaming and giving shape to my dream in poems and studies and sending out my thoughts to the Calcutta public through the magazines and other papers. You can well understand that it was a life quite different from the life of the West. I do not know if any of your Western poets or writers do pass the greatest part of their young days in such absolute seclusion.

I am almost certain that it cannot be possible and that seclusion itself has no place in the Western world.

'And my life went on like this. I was an obscure individual to most of my countrymen in those days. I mean that my name was hardly known outside my own province, but I was quite content with that obscurity, which protected me from the curiosity of the crowds.

'And then came a time when my heart felt a longing to come out of that solitude and to do some work for my human fellow-beings, and not merely give shapes to my dreams and meditate deeply on the problems of life, but try to give expression to my ideas through some definite work, some definite service for my fellow-beings.

'And the one thing, the one work which came to my mind was to teach children. It was not because I was specially fitted for this work of teaching, for I have not had myself the full benefit of a regular education. For some time I hesitated to take upon myself this task, but I felt that as I had a deep love for nature I had naturally love for children also. My object in starting the institution was to give the children of men full freedom of joy, of life and of communion with nature. I myself had suffered when young through the impediments which were inflicted upon most boys while they attended school and I have had to go through the machine of education which crushes the joy and freedom of life for which children have such insatiable thirst. And my object was to give freedom and joy to children of men.

'And so I had a few boys around me, and I taught them, and I tried to make them happy. I was their playmate. I was their companion. I shared their life, and I felt that I was the biggest child of the party. And we all grew up together in the atmosphere of freedom.

'The vigour and the joy of the children, their chats and songs filled the air with a spirit of delight, which I drank every day I was there. And in the evening during the sun-set hour I often used to sit alone watching the trees of the shadowing avenue, and in the silence of the afternoon I could hear distinctly the voices of the children coming up in the air, and it seemed to me that these shouts and songs and glad voices were like those trees, which come out from the heart of the earth like fountains of life towards the bosom of the infinite sky. And it symbolised, it brought before my mind the whole cry of human life, all expressions of joy and aspirations of men rising from the heart of Humanity up to this sky. I could see that, and I knew that we also, the grown-up children, send up our cries of aspiration to the Infinite. I felt it in my heart of hearts.

'In this atmosphere and this environment I used to write my poems Gitanjali, and I sang them to myself in the midnight under the glorious stars of the Indian sky. And in the early morning and in the afternoon glow of sun-set I used to write these songs till a day came when I felt impelled to come out once again and meet the heart of the large world.'

RABINDRANATH refused to go to school after the age of 14 and did not submit himself to a degree course or examination. But he spent a good deal of time in later life working to create the right kind of school, the right kind of university. He started and was the guiding spirit of the school of the passage; it was in the rural area of Santiniketan where too he founded and developed a University (fighting heroically for its funding into old age). Both institutions are now permanent and treasured parts of the West Bengal and Indian educational system; but the Tagorean approach is not so easily protected. In this as in so much that he did the person is irreplaceable: perhaps what makes a truly historical figure. To regard his life for a moment as a flow of creative power, it seems to shed a revelatory light on the capacities of the individual.

But he was human like the rest of us. There was an incident that is important in the history of Western critical work on Tagore, of which there has been very little. It is his reaction to a book published by Edward Thompson in 1926 (Oxford University Press), *Rabindranath Tagore: Poet and Dramatist*.

Thompson spent thirteen years preparing the book, for which he read all Tagore's poetry and plays to date in the original. He knew the poet personally and was his neighbour and colleague, teaching at another school, for ten years. His book was admired by some of Tagore's followers – P. N. Bishi, later head of the Department of Bengali at Calcutta University, called it a *hirak-ratna*, a diamond – but the poet's reaction was savage, belittling it mercilessly both to a friend in England in a private letter, and directly to the public in an article he published under a pseudonym. In my view Tagore probably had certain passages of the book pointed out to him that might well give offence if read on their own, and ignored the rest. Thompson's study is uneven; at times it is tactless and short-sighted; yet it is full of wonderful insights and the overall achievement is to present to the West a deep recognition of Tagore as a playwright of considerable standing and as one of the world's great lyric poets. I believe Tagore's actions were prompted in part by one or two of his friends who wanted to oust the young upstart – Thompson was a generation younger than the poet, and not afraid to show his opinion of slower-witted members of the inner circle. But the main reason for the rejection may have been a 'backlash' effect whereby the poet, having misrepresented himself in English and being unable to undo the damage, over-reacted at what he saw as another misrepresentation.

One may say – what damage? – since the translation had been so successful. But a letter of his to another English friend in 1935 seems to speak of deep and long-held reservations. 'As for myself, I ought never to have intruded into your realm of glory with my offerings hastily giving them a foreign shine and certain assumed gestures familiar to you. I have done thereby injustice to myself and the shrine of [the] Muse which proudly claims flowers from its own climate and culture. There is something humiliating in such an indecent hurry of impatient clamouring for one's immediate dues in wrong times and out of the way places.'

He wrote this in a mood of antipathy to the very idea of trans-lation of poetry, which passed over; but there is something rather more particular at work, a sense of self-betrayal in anxiety for Western recognition. However it may be, Edward Thompson was in disgrace and though there was a courteous and not unfriendly resumption of the relationship by letter, it was a slap in the face that he bore, however cheerfully, to the end of his days. It was quite out of character for Tagore. To Thompson's slightly anxious request for his opinion of an earlier version of the book, in 1921, he had replied, 'Never think that I am angry.' The book remains the only searching work in depth by a Westerner on Tagore, and my purpose in recalling the story here is mainly to recommend its merit, as it has suffered needlessly slighting comment since its summary rejection by the poet. Its latest belittling comes in a curiously back-handed way at the hands of Edward Thompson's son E. P. Thompson. *Alien Homage* (Oxford University Press, 1993) is an account by the historian of his father's interaction with Tagore and his work. The title tells us what the son makes of the business. With a kind of continuous damning with faint praise he shows his father as naïve, unable to see his cultural limitations, eager to praise the poet but not up to the job. Perhaps the title tells us too of a son unable to pay more than a doubtful tribute to a father. At all events it is time Edward Thompson's work was given something more like its due. Its scope is remarkable: as it follows the development of an oceanic talent it is blown hither and thither off course; yet the journey has something of greatness in it. Touched with blemish it is indeed a jewel of a book.

EDWARD THOMPSON was the first to translate Tagore's poetry into English in poetic form. He made a respectable job of it, using rhyme and metre in a craftsmanlike way. They are what I would call honest translations, justifying their unprosaic presentation on the page. The fresh and powerful river of the originals is reduced to a rivulet, an archaic rivulet at that, and yet its flow is true. Many Bengalis have learnt some Thompson at school and enjoyed it, remembering it with affection. (He did not tackle *Gitanjali*.) Since his time it has become fashionable to put down words with feeling and break them up somehow on the page and to call the result poetry. The dilution in content that has come to be accepted, of what word-vehicles in the poetic chain carry, has endangered the very life of poetry, while apparently making it easier to write and more popular than ever before.

For his later volumes of poetry Tagore himself used a loose-linked prosaic patterning to compelling effect. The ease of such an approach will itself contribute to the poetic truth of the whole – provided that, as with any form, it justifies its use. All real poetry uses a form or forms of its own, words with or without rhyme that take on an extra-prosaic strength from a persuasive delivery into the atmosphere. It is essentially a rhetorical device, arising from a skill in the organisation of the sounds of meaning. It has a beauty of its own and at the same time presents the prosaic meaning of the words as something deserving of that beauty, an accompaniment freed of the run-on haste of the prosaic format. The shaping force of the sentence is still used, if more lightly; but within a freedom of movement the form itself controls. The form establishes its own agreement with the mind of reader or audience and carries it along. There is scope for a far deeper possession of meaning. From the springboard of prose poetry leaps to a new use of words where the mind has all the time in the world to catch their effect before they disappear, cleanly, and the poem is over.

It is as if we have forgotten what poetry has always done. The belly-flop charade of the modern scene, West and East it seems, has its effect on translators too. If a poetic format is adopted, a presentation of words on the page that draws attention to itself by its otherness from the prose-paragraph, that says in effect 'I am a poem' – then the very form or shape it takes should persuade from the moment of take-off to the disappearance of the final syllable. It is the credibility gap in mid-air control, as it were, that sinks poetry and its translation, and if the art cannot be managed, then better to follow the ground-plan of prose.

This is what Rabindranath did in his translations. He knew he was not a poet in English and was not one to practise the confidence trick of semi-control; he was a writer who delivered. And so he elaborated his prose versions.

Prose with a poetic touch and refrain-like repetition allows something of the beauty of the original to come across. There is something else, of the oratory of prose, that has its own appeal. The voice the outside world came to know the *Gitanjali* by was magical, compelling; for a moment it was on everyone's lips; then silenced in Time. A more faithful rendering of the poems in itself offers no magic. Yet if a virtue of poetry is at work, and the imagination given its freedom, then there will be time and space for the great song of the *Gitanjali* as if from a distance to be heard. Its theme, to borrow a phrase of Tagore's from elsewhere, is 'the play of love between God and the human soul'. Let Edward Thompson then, the poet's first Western interpreter, introduce the collection here. 'The poems were written to be sung; but they sing themselves.'

JOE WINTER
Calcutta, October 1997

Song Offerings

GITANJALI

I

O now beneath your feet's dust let
    my head kneel on the ground.
Yield up my arrogance to tears,
    let all my pride be drowned.
If glory to myself I offer
it is self-insult that I suffer –
and then I die within myself,
    turning around, around.
Yield up my arrogance to tears,
    let all my pride be drowned.

Let me not advertise myself
    in various things I do –
but let my deeds fit your desire,
    that your will may come through.
O for your true peace is my longing,
and your dear image's belonging.
Within my heart of lotus petal
    may your shield be found.
Yield up my arrogance to tears,
    let all my pride be drowned.

2

Many and deep my cravings are
    which you denying, unwaveringly
store up the blessings in my life
        by saving me.
Without my asking you have given
body, mind, life; light in sky's heaven.
To fitness for these marvellous gifts
    most slowly you are moving me,
from danger of too-great desires
        delivering me.

Sometimes I err – and sometimes follow
    along your path unswervingly,
at which you vanish, as if still
        reproving me.
O yet it is your loving way
of welcome, to turn me away.
To fitness for a life fulfilled,
    your union, you are moving me,
from danger of too-weak desires
        delivering me.

3

Making the unknown known, allowing
    in home after home a place for me —
you bring the far to near, my friend,
        make strangers brotherly.
The fearful step has seemed immense
that leaves an old known residence . . .
that you are old amidst the new
    is what I easily do not see.
You bring the far to near, my friend,
        make strangers brotherly.

Through life, through death, through the far worlds,
    whenever, wherever guiding me on,
O you aware of my birth beyond time —
    you make all known, at one.
With you no stranger can appear,
no barrier can exist, no fear.
O you awake in the union of all —
    forever to see you, let it so be.
You bring the far to near, my friend,
        make strangers brotherly.

4

In danger save me — such a prayer
   is not of my heart's choosing,
      but that in danger I stay free from fear.
In sorrow's throes O let me
   rather your solace losing,
      uplift myself, not drown in sorrow's tear.
If support is sought and taken
my own strength may snap and weaken.
When all the savage fraudulent world
   offers is a refusing —
      then in my mind let no defeat come near.

Afford protection — such a prayer
   is not of my heart's choosing,
      but that my power to come through may appear.
In heaviness O let me
   rather your solace losing,
      not lightened be, but carry a burden clear.
Though your face, through my lowered eyes
in days of joy I recognise . . .
when in the night of pain I see
   the whole world's harsh refusing —
      O let my trust in you not disappear.

5

O you who know heart's deeper power,
    make my heart flower.
O make it pure and shining-true,
    and beautiful too.
Thrill it awake, from soul's sleep save –
    O make it brave.
From doubts and laziness free
        so let it lovely be.
O you who know heart's deeper power,
    make my heart flower.

O let its oneness with all people deepen,
    my closed heart open.
Let all its deeds lead on from your calm rhythm,
    serenely driven.
O at your lotus feet let my heart lie
    untremblingly.
And let its delight all be
        to delight delightedly.
O you who know heart's deeper power,
    make my heart flower.

6

In love life song smell light and ecstasy
your elixir cascading steadily
    has flooded all the Earth and all the skies.
In such forms purest joy, finding a way
to shatter what is shut throughout, today
    to a life that's nectar-filled has given rise.

My consciousness, fresh-drenched in showering light,
has opened like a lotus in delight . . .
    its honey-richness all at your feet lies.
Now visiting the outskirts of the heart
the splendid sun has risen of day's start,
    drawing a curtain from the lazy eyes.

7

Into my life come new, come new,
in smell, in colour, in song too;
come in body, come in mind;
come in touch of thrilling kind;
in joy, in sleep's spell come: O you
into my life come new, come new.

Come the beautiful, bright and graceful,
the pure and splendid, and the peaceful;
in form of vast and various law;
in pain, in pleasure, and at heart's core.
Come in all daily tasks: O you
come at the end of what we do . . .
into my life come new, come new.

8

Today I'll watch the paddy play
    hide-and-seek in shadow-light.
Who has floated in the blue sky
    a boat of cloud so white?
        Today wild-circling in the sky,
        its honey forgotten, a bee whirls by.
        Today by the river why should a crowd
        of *chokha-chokhi* birds alight?

Hey, I'm not going home today brother,
    brother, I'll stay outside!
Hey, let's break the sky open today
    and plunder it far and wide!
        As if with tide-foam lifting and straying
        on the breeze, and laughing, and never still staying –
        today all idle, with some flute-playing
        the time will pass till night.

9

From joy's loveliest ocean
    there's a flood springing.
Embark all, and set to —
    to the oar your strength bringing.
        No matter its burden,
        our boat sorrow-laden
        (if death comes, so let it)
            moves through the waves winging.
        From joy's loveliest ocean
            there's a flood springing.

Who cries from behind us
    of doubt or of danger?
Who harps on their fear now,
    where fear is no stranger?
        What curse, or stars' showing
        has frowned on our going?
        Hoist a sail to the wind now
            and we'll move on singing.
        From joy's loveliest ocean
            there's a flood springing.

10

Today my tears of sorrow are
    your dish of gold's adorning;
        a necklace will be strung for you of pearl.
At your feet, dearest Mother,
    the moon and sun are spinning
        a wreath of light; and at your heart a jewel
is of my sorrow shining.

Such splendid estate is yours! then tell me,
    with such a fortune, what you will be doing.
        Allow me some, or take more, at your pleasure.
Sorrow is my home truth. That you
    afford your grace for it – even as if buying –
        O you who know the true from worthless treasure –
this is my pride of being.

II

We have tied *kash*-stalks together, we have wound
    the *sephali*-flower in garlands. We have crowned
        wicker-trays with new paddy, carrying them.

Come
    dear Lakshmi of Autumn
        in your pure white chariot of cloud
            down the clear blue road;
come in glittering light, washed-clean
    of mountain-forest-green;
        come in white-lotus-chaplet,
            cool-dew-wet.

Where *malati*-flowers have fallen
    your seat is spread in a secluded garden
        at the risen Ganga's side.
Swans are circling wide-
    stretched, ready at your foot's station
        to lay wing beside.

Now from your golden *bina*'s strings
    let murmuring songs
        arise; and a sweet, controlled, loud playing;
and melody pouring
    in laughter, quick-melting
        in a tear-stream's soft lilting.

As at times the philosopher's-stone blazes
   from the edge of your drifting tresses –
      for an instant so with your kind hand
touch touch my mind . . .
      and my thoughts all to gold will come,
         dark light become.

12

The pure white sail of the boat is struck
    by a soft sweet blowing.
My eyes have never seen before
    the spell of this boat's going.
    From what sea's launching is the boat,
      with what far treasure laden?
    My mind simply wants to float –
to leave all wants behind on the near shore,
      with all material burden.

At the cloud's back in a rush of rain
    tumbles the cry of thunder.
Still the sunshine falls on my face,
    through cloud-bits chopped asunder.
    Hey, Mister Boatman, who are you, hey –
      with your treasure of tears and laughter?
    I'm dying to know, what melody
will you set your instrument to today,
      what hymn will follow after?

13

My eyes' enchantress, you are here.
With open heart I see you clear,
in heaps of flowers all fallen free
on ground around the *siuli*-tree.
From dew-wet grass to dew-wet grass
with red feet of the dawn you pass.
Eyes' enchantress, you are here.

Your scarf composed of shadow-light
through forest-leaf is slipping, straying;
as flowers gaze upon the sight
of that face – what can they be saying?
For our part we will welcome you;
but let the cloud-screen disappear,
the veil that keeps your face from view:
with both hands take it, thrust it clear . . .
eyes' enchantress, you are here.

Before the forest-goddess' dwelling,
at its entrances and doors,
I hear the conch's deep note swelling.
And your song of welcome soars
from *bina*-strings set in sky's sphere.

Where do the golden anklets ring?
At heart I hear a dancing tone
in all I do, in everything.
Pouring the honey that can melt stone,
eyes' enchantress, you are here.

14

Mother, today in the pale early light your sad feet I behold,
Mother, stealing across the sky a death-stealing truth is told.

O I touch your feet in all the world's to-do.
O I touch your feet in all my life may do.

Today I offer body mind wealth for an incense-stick to hold,
O saviour of devotion, in your temple-space untold.
Mother, today in the pale early light your sad feet I behold.

15

Into the cosmos as a whole
    a song of joy is freed.
O when into my very soul
    will it strike deep indeed?
        Wind and water, light and sky —
        to love these, so that they troop by
        at my heart's court all variously,
           shall I once succeed?

When, at my eyes' new-opening,
    shall I be glad at heart?
To be of some small use to all,
    down which road shall I start?
        That you are here — O when will this be
        sure within my life and easy?
        When of itself will your true name
           echo within each deed?

16

Cloud on cloud has gathered,
  dark is coming near.
Why am I in the doorway?
  Why do you keep me here?
    With many tasks of the working day,
    the many people with whom I stay,
    I find myself sitting alone
      intent that you'll appear.
    Why am I in the doorway?
      Why do you keep me here?

If you don't reveal yourself,
  but use me with disdain,
how then shall I manage
  in the coming time of rain?
    Into the distance I strain my eyes
    and only stare – as my heart cries,
    weeping as the wayward wind
      disturbs the atmosphere.
    Why am I in the doorway?
      Why do you keep me here?

17

Where is the light? Where, where is the light?
With separation's torch set it alight.
    A lamp with no flame's crest – is this
    the fate set down I shall not miss?
Even to die is better than that, more bright.
With separation's torch give my lamp light.

The messenger of grief sings, 'For your sake
O Life, on your account God is awake.
    When pitch-black dark of night is falling
    to a love-tryst he is calling,
rich-honouring you by way of sorrow's ache.
O Life, on your account God is awake.'

Clouds in layer on layer have massed and deepened.
Rain is pouring down, the heavens have opened.
    And that my heart is suddenly
    awake this awful night – O tell me,
can you tell me why this should have happened?
Rain is pouring down, the heavens have opened.

The lustre is soon lost of lightning's spark.
It leaves the eyes cloaked in a deeper dark.
    I don't know where it is, the song
    of deep note that draws me along,
or how far off, that still is my life's mark.
It leaves the eyes cloaked in a deeper dark.

Where is the light? Where, where is the light?
With separation's torch set it alight.
　　Clouds are thundering, a storm-wind blowing,
　　the passage of time will stop my going
in this dense dark, this deepest dead of night.
With my life set the lamp of love alight.

18

Today in the dark baffling light
   of *Srabon*'s deepening cloud-haze,
you stole upon your way like night
   escaping everybody's gaze.
      You came when morning's eye was closed,
      its brazen blue no more exposed.
      Now wind calls vainly under cover,
      for someone has spread thick cloud over.

The birds are silent in the groves.
   The door is closed to every home.
On the road no traveller moves –
   the road on which you lonely roam.
      O dear friend, as you pass before
      my house-front, see the open door!
      O lonely journeyer on dream's flow,
      shouldering me aside, don't go!

19

Asharh's dusk comes.
    Day's surge is gone.
An uncontained rain-drift
    pours on and on.
        What does the wind say
        in the forest of the *juthi*-flower?
        What's here for my thoughts
            to focus upon?
        An uncontained rain-drift
            pours on and on.

Waves rise in my heart.
    I'm lost, my strength's spent.
I find myself weeping
    at the wet *juthi*'s scent.
        With what tune shall I fill up
        this dark night? Forgetful,
        unsure, what life's error
            have I undergone?
        An uncontained rain-drift
            pours on and on.

20

Tonight in storm to a lovers' meeting
     (O my friend, friend of my heart)
you seek a way. The sky is weeping;
and I unsleeping, vigil keeping.
     Again and again to the door I start
     (O my friend, friend of my heart).

I look outside. Your journey's going
all unseen, is past my knowing.
   By forest-cover coming over,
   or on the bank of a distant river,
     or in thick darkness set apart,
   you are crossing to your lover
     (O my friend, friend of my heart).

21

Beloved, from some old time, I know
you have cast me adrift upon life's flow.
All at once I find, wherever I go
    a gift, the spirit's soaring.

From behind cloud so many days
you have stepped — as the sun with laughter's rays
a blessing on my forehead lays,
    your sweetest touch restoring.

In so many moments, so many years,
so much that is new, in so many spheres,
in glimpses of form, the formless appears,
    such light in these eyes storing.

From age to age, no-one knows how long,
happiness, sorrow, love and song
have risen in the heart brim-full and strong,
    such rain of nectar pouring.

22

Maestro your song is such as to astound.
Dumbstruck I only listen to the sound.
    Its melody-light fits the world as a cover;
    through the heavens its air is carried over;
        bursting through rock a tumultuous river
           streams out to make a melody of the ground.

I imagine I am singing to that note –
and find my tune is lost within my throat.
    My words halt in their wished-for phrasing –
    my heart weeps at the defeat it's facing . . .
        you have trapped me in a melody's embracing,
           flinging its net around me, far around.

23

To hide like this and cover yourself away,
              it will not do.
Hide in my heart – if I don't mention it,
                 then who will, who?
          This game of hide-and-seek you're playing,
          from this to that land shifting, staying . . .
now say that you'll be captured – and I beg,
              no tricks from you!
To hide like this and cover yourself away,
              it will not do.

    My friend, I know my heart's a place
    too hardened for your feet to grace . . .
yet if you touch there, will your spirit's breath
              not melt it through?

    And if I search and strive no more –
    still as your grains of mercy pour,
will suddenly flowers forget to break out, fruit
             not ripen too?
To hide like this and cover yourself away,
              it will not do.

24

Not to have seen you, Lord, in the day
of my life, not to find you . . . must itself stay
   in the mind's keeping.
I may not forget, the pain will hurt yet,
   awake and sleeping.

I have grasped with both hands whatever I may
from the world, finding wealth in time's outlay . . .
yet that I have nothing, must itself stay
   in the mind's keeping.
I may not forget, the pain will hurt yet,
   awake and sleeping.

If I too lazily sit by the way,
if I make my bed in the road's dust, say . . .
that all the road waits, must itself stay
   in the mind's keeping.
I may not forget, the pain will hurt yet,
   awake and sleeping.

Laughter may rise, the flute may play,
the house may fill with a grand display . . .
but that you are absent, must itself stay
   in the mind's keeping.
I may not forget, the pain will hurt yet,
   awake and sleeping.

25

Always I see your sorrow-of-absence.
 Every world-wide place,
forest and mountain, sky and sea
 mirrors it in new face.
  Silent, steady-eyed in the throng
  of stars it stands in place night-long.
  Petal and leaf reflect its song;
   and *Srabon*'s rain-stream-race.

  In every home it can amass
  such pain, in so much love, alas,
  so much desire, joy, grief, work as
   it deepens its sad trace.

  All life is vacant as it spills
  its song and through all forms distils.
  O now your sorrow-of-absence fills
   my own heart's empty space.

26

Day is no more. Shadow has fallen
      dark and low.
I need to fill the pitcher at the stream,
      it's time to go.
   Dusk is restless in the sky
   with the water gurgling by.
   O I am called to on the path
     by that loud flow!
I need to fill the pitcher at the stream,
      it's time to go.

The path is lonely now, all bare
      of coming and going.
O in the river of love the waves have risen,
     a quick wind's blowing!
   If I'll come back I cannot say.
   Who is it I will meet today?
   Someone is playing the *bina* in a boat
    whom I don't know.
I need to fill the pitcher at the stream,
      it's time to go.

27

Today at monsoon's height the torrent pours
        continuously.
What check can it have, the stream's sky-breaking
        urgency?
    Over a forest of wild *shaal*-leaves
    the storm thunderously swings and heaves —
    as across a field the water weaves
        all crazily.
Today, whirling cloud-tufts away,
        who's dancing free?

Hey, the storm has swept over my mind —
        it's a free-for-all!
But these waves overflowing my heart,
        at whose feet do they fall?
    With what an uproar am I shaken —
    at every door the bolt is broken —
    in the monsoon a madness is woken
        deep in me!
Who's charging about, inside and out,
        on a drunken spree?

28

Lord, for you my eyes unclosed today.
     They do not see
          but only look upon the way.
     Even that is dear to me.

Sitting in dust outside your door
my heart asks that from your rich store
     an offering it may acquire –
          a beggar's plea.
               It does not find it, but desire:
     even that is dear to me.

All who share this world with me
so busily, so happily
     have gone ahead – and there is none
          with whom to be.
               To long for One –
     even that is dear to me.

The earth, from all directions seen
is filled with sweetness; eager; green . . .
     I weep for love of it. Again again
          unseeingly
               I feel the pain.
     Even that is dear to me.

29

Alas, society, wealth draw me apart . . .
and yet you know I long for you at heart.
   O you who know me better than I do, seeing
   what is within, O Lord, who know my being –
   as sorrow, joy, forgetfulness impart –
      indeed you know I long for you at heart.

My pride I cannot set down and abandon,
but veer round desperate with its head-burden.
What happiness – if it and I could part!
   In truth you know I long for you at heart.

      When every single thing of mine shall fall
      into your hands – you will, by taking all,
      be mine in all, when from all I depart.
         For my heart longs for you at heart, at heart!

30

Dear one, this is your love,
   O my heart-thief.
A golden-hued dancing light
   over a leaf;
      a honey-cloud upon the sky
      floating thoroughly lazily by;
      a breeze breathing about the body
        its nectar-relief; –
      dear one, this is your love,
        O my heart-thief.

A stream of dayspring-light
   flood-fills my eyes.
This your message of love
   in my soul lies.
      Here is your face before my sense –
      saluted by that countenance,
      I touch now in heart's reverence
        your feet in brief.

31

I live for one reason only,
    Lord, to sing your song.
In the world's court of your followers
    so let me belong.
        My life has been idle, playing
        tunes of no account, delaying
        all its vital task, yet staying
          in your living throng.

In the night-filled quiet temple
    of your praise, O king,
I receive divine instruction,
    your command – to sing.
        Let this honour then be given –
        to be near, while in dawn-heaven
        the *bina*'s notes pour steady-golden.
        Lord, for this I long.

32

O break it down, break down my fear.
Turn your face round towards me here.
    How do I know it if from beside?
    What do I see – this side, that side?
    O you who play with my heart and hide,
        look smilingly straight at it, clear.

Speak to me, speak your word to me,
   and take my body in your grip.
O stretch out your right hand to me,
   take hold of me and raise me up.
    What I see is wrong and wrong my seeking.
    False is my laughter, false my weeping.
    Before me now your presence keeping,
       O let all falsehood disappear.

33

Again the crowd at my heart dashes and flies.
Again the screen comes down before my eyes.
    Again the words all pile up in my brain,
    my soul in all directions scurries in vain,
    and I have lost your holy presence again,
        as flames of anguish prosper still and rise.

Your silent truth that under my heart lies,
O may it not be drowned in people's cries.
    In all the busy throng with me remain.
    Within your being O shield me and contain —
    and in my knowing mind always sustain
        the three worlds and their open, light-filled skies.

34

Since you began your way to me
    how long it has been!
Where will your moon, your sun in shining
    still be your screen?
For so many dawns and dusks of time
your footsteps rang out in their chime,
and in my heart your messenger called
    going there unseen.

O dear traveller, today
    it is as if
joy shiveringly had broken out
    upon my life –
and that perhaps today the time has come,
and that whatever work was mine is done.
O great king, fragrance-charged with you a wind
    arrives, is keen.

35

Dense and soaking, O come
    in the clouds' rain-drive;
in the grandeur of tender green
    to where I am alive, –
        in the mountain-peak you embrace,
        the shadow-rich thicket-place,
        or in thunder that all sky-space
            will deafen and rive.

Rising in labour, *neepo*-trees
    floweringly thrill;
over the river-banks the sobbing
    waters spill:
        O come, into my spirit flow,
        come, rob me of my deep thirst, O
        come close, intense, eye-cooling, so
            now at my heart arrive.

36

Will you let your life go as in a leaf-shaking,
     dropping away, floating away,
in the rhythm of joy and the joy of breaking?
With your ear to the ground don't you hear all around
    the tune of death on death's *bina* waking,
in stars, sun and moon as you rush forward soon –
    O what joy of it – to the fire to be lit,
      to that flame-making?

    As you listen to that maddening song
    who knows where the rushing-along
is bound that will not turn and look round
and is not to be found in a knot tightly wound
    but shoots on past as it loots quick and fast
      with joy in what it is taking!

    As these footsteps of joy advance
    the six seasons dance their abandoned dance,
and all the world's ground is in a flood drowned
of colour song smell in Earth's pell-mell
    in a throwing-away, in a giving-away,
      in joy of life's forsaking!

37

The dream of night has run, has run —
the chain is now undone, undone.
Life's barrier has ceased to be:
into the world I am set free.
In the lotus-petals of my heart
    a blossoming has begun, begun.

You came up to my door, stood fast,
and it was broken down at last.
My heart's obeisance at your feet
    now tearfully is done, is done.

The light of morning-time descends
and to me now its hand it lends.
Across my broken prison-gate
    a shout comes that has won, has won!

38

In Autumn now at the spirit's door
    who has come to stay?
O my heart, a song of joy, of delight
    let us sing today.
The silent words of the sky's blue,
the feverish eagerness of the dew,
today upon your *bina*'s strings
    let all these play.

To the golden song of a field of grain
may our song add a like refrain;
and down a river's full pure notes
    float on its way.

Someone is here. Let our eyes rest
with deep content on the face of the guest,
as in new company out-of-doors
    we wander and stray.

39

All I wish is to sing it, the song
    I have come here to sing.
But I only practise the tunes. There is no
    song-offering.

It has not found me, the song, nor have I
    divined its word —
yet all my life at heart is a wish
    for the song to be heard.
Still there is only a breeze on the air,
    the flower does not spring.

I have not seen that person come, nor have I
    heard the profound
truth of those lips; but I hear only
    the footsteps' sound
going back and forth at times outside my door,
    not entering.

Only a place to be seated, all through the day
    is waiting within.
The lamp has not been lit. How shall I call
    that person in?
I long for our being-at-one . . . but this room knows of
    no such thing.

40

How long shall I sit and guard
   this perishable store?
O Lord, thinking, thinking at night
   I can stay awake no more.
      Whoever wants to come, throughout
      the night and day I shut him out,
      as in suspicion and in doubt
        I chase him from the door.

To my lonely room then not a soul
   a visit pays.
Meanwhile, Lord, on the outside
   your world happily plays.
      Yet you too may not find a way,
      but come and have to turn away.
      What I want to keep, that too won't stay . . .
        and all is dust on the floor.

41

Now cast aside these dark-stained clothes,
    my heart, it shall be done.
The self that clothes me is a deep-stained one.
    As through the day's dust it has toiled
    by mark on mark it has been spoiled;
    while self-pride scorches in a heat
      that's scarcely undergone.
The self that clothes me is a deep-stained one.

      Now at last all toil is over
        in the day's unforming.
      Hope in my life I discover
        at His certain coming.
    O come and bathe, for it is time –
      and put love's raiment on.
    Now from evening's forest-garden
    gather flowers and weave a garland.
Come O come, for all the time has gone.

42

Joy thrills all my body,
    my eyes are dazed and hot.
Who has fastened up my heart
    with a red *rakhi*-knot?
        How is it beneath this sky,
        this water land flower fruit nearby,
        there's such heart's increase? – tell me why,
            O heart-thief, I know not.

What game is it that today
    I play with you here?
Have I found? – do I still seek? –
    it is all unclear.
        If joy needs excuse to weep,
        it is that this pain – to keep
        sweet separation, rising steep
            has flooded my heart's plot.

43

Don't cover up your right hand, Lord;
    leave it free instead.
I have come to you today
      to tie the *rakhi*-thread.
         If I tie it on your wrist,
         to all and with all who exist
         today I will be joined as one,
            as if brother-wed.

Today let all distinction go
    between the world and me.
At home, outside, your equal being
      O Lord, may I see.
         Now our distance disappears
         in which I circle round in tears:
         and for an instant now to you
            my joyful cry is sped.

44

At the world's rite of joy a guest,
my human life is blessed, is blessed.
  In the city of beautiful forms
  my sight each flickering wish performs,
  as by sweet notes profound my hearing
      is possessed.

At the sacred flame you duties name:
  the flute I play,
and tell in songs the story of tears
  and laughter's play.
    Is the time now? I see you gain
    your great court. Now I shall sustain
    your victory-note. And my heart's-offering
      is expressed.

45

Light-flooding with light you came here, light of light.
The non-light lifts: my eyes are freed of night.
    With all the sky and all the earth
    lit with delight, with laughter's birth —
whatever my eyes light on, all is good and fine and right.

On the tree's leaf a dance is born and lives in your light's
                                          freeing.
In the bird's nest your light summons a song into its being.
    And at my body lovingly
    your light has fallen over me,
and at my heart your pure hand I have felt alight, alight!

46

Prostrate, Lord, on the ground at your throne-seat,
I shall be ashen with the dust of your feet.
    Why set me up in honour at a distance?
        O my whole life use not with this deceit,
    but draw me in dishonour to your presence.
        I shall be ashen with the dust of your feet.

At the back of your band of pilgrims I shall go.
O let my place be lowest of the low.
    So many run to take your blessings' store —
        I'll taste what's left, when their wants are complete.
    Till then I shall not hunger, but adore.
        I shall be ashen with the dust of your feet.

47

I have dived deep in the ocean of beauty,
    a pearl past beauty to come by.
My drifting damaged boat no longer
      between this harbour and that will ply.
        Let me finally discover
        the pummelling of the waves is over . . .
      now as I succumb to nectar
        I become deathless as I die.

There is a song that is not for the ear
    and where that song eternally sounds,
I shall advance with the *bina* of life
      into a court that has no bounds.
        I shall make the song of eternity,
        its weeping my last melody;
      and at the foot of the silent One
        the silent *bina* then shall lie.

48

Under the heavens now has bloomed
　　light's lotus-flower.
The many petals in their hundreds
outwards inwards backwards forwards
have covered the black lake of darkness
　　with their power.
Brother, in a golden room
I joyful sit amidst the bloom
that spreads out slowly and unfolds
　　light's lotus-flower.

In the heavens all on a wave
　　wind freely blows.
In all directions is a song,
on all sides life quick-dances along;
a certain touch has filled the sky
　　that my whole body knows.
Diving into the living sea
I take in life till it fills me, –
while shifting round as it surrounds
　　wind freely blows.

On all ten sides, laying down her shawl
　　Earth offers her lap.
To each and every thing that lives
she calls, and as all come, she gives

the food of life, to each her richness
    offering up.
A fragrant song has my heart filled:
I sit in joy's great circling, thrilled
as round me, laying down her shawl
    Earth offers her lap.

Light, I kneel to you, from all my sin
    grant my releasing.
Upon my forehead touch and keep
    a father's blessing.
Wind, I kneel to you, from my fatigue
    allow my easing.
Let all my body lightly feel
    a father's blessing.
Earth, I kneel to you, may my heart's wish
    find its rejoicing.
Make ripen, till it fill the house,
    a father's blessing.

49

Here one has arranged her lap
 in the house we share.
Brother, a fit place for her
 devotedly prepare.
First sweep all the dust away
 with a song of love.
Secondly the rubbish-bits
 carefully remove.
Next put flowers in the basket,
 sprinkling water there.
Brother, a fit place for her
 devotedly prepare.

She is present day and night
 in the house we share.
In the morning with her laughter
 light pours on the air.
The moment we wake up at dawn,
 open our eyes and see,
we can see her looking back
 at us happily.
The house is filled with her, as if
 her kindly look to wear.
In the morning with her laughter
 light pours on the air.

Sometimes, too, she sits alone
    in the house we share,
when we all have tasks to do
    and must go elsewhere.
She goes with us to the door
    and sees us on our way,
and lightly then and with a song
    at heart we go away.
When at day's end, tasks all done,
    homewards we repair,
we see her sitting here alone
    in the house we share.

She is sitting here awake
    in the house we share,
when we lie upon the bed,
    thoughtless, in sleep's care.
The lamp she holds is hidden, seen
    by no-one at all.
As it burns the whole night through
    she shades it with her shawl.
As our dreams go back and forth
    on sleep's thoroughfare,
she is smiling in the dark
    in the house we share.

50

God of the silent soul
   awake, alone,
today I will open a door
    and be known.

Whom do I seek all day
   in the swift outside?
I will learn the holy word
    of eventide.

I light the lamp of my life
   with your life's light.
O priest, in quiet I will make
    my gift tonight.

Where the cosmos has taught
   a world to pray,
I too of that radiance
    will hold a ray.

51

What light kindling your lamp of life
    brings you here to the world?
Dear saint, dear lunatic, dear lover
    you are here in the world.

In this home that has no bounds
the *bina* of sorrow, of hurt in your being sounds.
    In your deepest danger
who is the mother before whose smile you have smiled?

In search of whom do you go,
all comfort flung to the flames? Who can know?
    Who makes you weep in despair
whom your heart in such desperate love to itself has held?

Nothing stays you, no cause.
Who is your heart's companion? this gives me pause.
    Oblivious of death
to what endless ocean of life do you joyfully yield?

52

You are my own: where I am you are too.
    O may this be said and granted the saying of it.
The full delight of my life is all in you.
    O may this be said and granted the saying of it.

Within my speech may sweetness be,
let nectar fill my melody.
You are my dearest O may this word
    be said and granted the saying of it.

With your presence you immerse
the sky and earth and universe.
From my heart O may this word
    be said and granted the saying of it.

You see one low and come before
that one with love as he is poor.
With my poor voice O may this word
    be said and granted the saying of it.

53

Bring me down to your feet,
    O bring me down!
Let my life float in tears,
    O melt my heart!
I am alone with pride's
    immovable crown.
Reduce to dust this stone seat,
    smash it apart!
Bring me down to your feet,
    O bring me down!

What can I find to vaunt
    of my failed day?
Though the house is full I am nought
    with you away.
In its own depths the day's work
    all will drown.
O may it tell, the worship
    at sundown.
Bring me down to your feet,
    O bring me down!

54

Today in the scent-laden air
   whom do I seek between the trees?
Beneath the blue sky's troubled stare
   what is this sobbing on the breeze?
      A song of sadness through and through
      visits my mind, my actions too
      from far. For whom does my heart seek
         in today's scent-laden air?

The tender song to which a young heart
   thrills alert . . . what can it be
O my dear one? The new leaves' cadence,
   the scent of the young-mango tree,
      the sky bathed with the moon-rays' sweetness,
      bring tears of pure delight to me.
      Whose blissful touch do I feel there,
         in today's scent-laden air?

55

Spring is awake at the door today.
Don't provoke or play your tricks
by hiding your veiled life away.
    Open the heart's-flower on its stem,
    forget, forget the 'us-and-them';
    in the song-vociferous sky
    let your fragrance wave-coast by;
    make free with every ounce of sweetness,
    in the wide world losing your way.

O what a deep hurt of the forest
sings in its tender greenery!
Waiting for whom on his way from the sky
does the Earth swarm into her finery?
    Now as the south wind through my heart pours,
    for whom has there been a knocking-at-doors?
    Who wakes the fragrance-bewildered night,
    as on the Earth his feet alight?
    O beautiful lover and lord, to whom
    is your solemn invitation, pray?

56

Down from the lion-seat throne
    your way you made –
and at the entrance to my lonely room
    you stood, Lord, and stayed.
        Alone in my own world
            a song I was singing,
        and as your hearing caught the melody
            your way you made –
        and at the entrance to my lonely room
            you stood, Lord, and stayed.

In your court are so many songs,
    so many fine minstrels –
today it was an unskilled song that drew
    your love's great accolade.
        For when to the universal melody
            was added a sad tune,
        then taking in your hands a crowning garland
            your way you made –
        and at the entrance to my lonely room
            you stood, Lord, and stayed.

57

Take me, Lord, take hold of me:
do not go back this time but stay
   and keep me in captivity.
The old time of your being away
I do not long for. Let that day
    depart all dustily.
May life, that's spread with your light, be
    awake continually.

To what compulsion did I yield?
What did I say in road and field
   as I roamed free?
O now your true word to me say.
Now may I cherish on my way
    your presence inwardly.

So much for which I am to blame,
so much evasiveness, heart's-shame
    still in its secrecy
beckons me back – O now in flame
    consume it utterly.

58

When life is all wrung out and dry,
    in an impulse of kindness, come.
When all that is sweet is snatched from the eye,
    in a note of song's nectar, come.
        And when work roaring-vast wave-slides
        overwhelmingly on all sides,
        to the edge of the heart with your silent feet
        come, Lord of peace, come.

When in its narrow corner the mind
is to its own mean self confined,
then through the door, O generous Lord
    in your kingly splendour, come.
        When the infinite dust of desire makes play
        to blind the fool and lead him astray –
        O pure One, O unsleeping One,
        with the light of destruction, come.

59

O silence him now, your poet
    of words that race;
take his heart's-flute, and play it
    with deepest grace.
In the night's depth let it sound
with a melody profound,
the flute-song with which you astound
    the worlds of space.

Whatever in life and death is flung
    about of me,
may this tune draw it to your feet
    in harmony.
The clutter of words of day on day
in an eye-blink will float away,
and I shall hear the flute play, in
    night's endless place.

60

In sky's blind darkness when the world
    in sleep is drowned,
who offers to my *bina*'s strings
    a thrilling sound?
Sleep is snatched away then and there.
I quit my bed and stare and stare:
and yet there is no person where
    my eyes gaze round.

As music's many murmurings
    through my heart flow,
what great truth moves the eager strings
    I do not know.
This heart's weight, tearful agony
I do not understand in me –
nor who it is whom I would see
    with my wreath crowned.

61

He came and sat beside me, and yet did not
      break my rest.
Unlucky girl, locked in a powerful
      sleep's arrest!
In silent night his way he made
and in his hands a *bina* played,
who later with deep singing left me
      dream-possessed.

I wake and a south wind is madly
      making free.
Its fragrance drifts and fills the darkness
      all round me.
O why does my night disappear?
Close he is yet he's not here.
Why can't I feel my true love's garland
      on my breast?

62

Haven't you heard his footsteps on the way?
    He is coming, he is coming, he is coming.
In every age and moment, night and day
    he is coming, he is coming.
        In each and every song I have sung
        (all to myself with mad jabbering tongue)
        it is of his arrival that all the notes play.
          He is coming, coming, coming.

For so many aeons on *Phalgun*-forest-ways
    he is coming, he is coming.
Cloud-chariot-drawn down so many *Srabon*-dark-days
    he is coming, he is coming.
        In perfect sorrow pure and whole
        his very feet are at my soul.
        O when with his light glad touch may
        the philosopher's-stone come into play,
          all to gold transforming?
            He is coming, coming, coming.

63

I surrender, surrender!
I thrust you away and wound myself,
    a self-offender.
        I cannot bear it — over and over
        I know this yet I re-discover —
        that in my mind's sky someone will cover
            and hide your splendour.

My past life shadow-like pursues,
    clinging behind.
How much its flute-song conjures with
    enchantment blind!
        But here's the quick resolving chord:
        I let your arms catch me, O Lord;
        and what of me in life is stored
            at your door I tender.

64

Discard your used strings one by one,
    and where the spaces are
tie up the new strings on the old *sitar*.
       A courtly gathering
       will soon sit listening
    in dusk to one for whom the time has come
    to play a farewell tune to day's bazaar.
       Tie up the new strings on the old *sitar*.

O my dear open your door to me
    upon the sky and night
and let the silence of the seven worlds
    at your house alight.
       Now let the ending of the song
       arrive that you have sung so long.
    And that this instrument is indeed your own,
    even let this from your knowing vanish far.
       Tie up the new strings on the old *sitar*.

65

When did I burst out singing your song? –
    indeed it is not today, today.
When did my heart begin to long? –
    indeed it is not today, today.
        A waterfall into the open flowing
        of its quest is all unknowing:
        so then on life's stream came I rushing,
           carried along –
indeed it is not today, today.

So many names I called him by, painted
so many pictures, all unacquainted
        with where he whom I joyfully sought
          might stay and belong –
indeed it is not today, today.

Just as a flower waiting for light
unwittingly stays awake all night,
        so hopes of you round my waiting heart
        cluster and throng –
indeed it is not today, today.

66

To bear the burden of your love
    is more than I can do.
Therefore in this worldly home,
    clear between us two,
you have seen to it, O Lord,
    a great screen should be
of joy grief honour people wealth
    set down mercifully.
From behind this, now and then
    you let yourself be seen
in hints, as mild rays of the sun
    pierce a black cloud-screen.
The one you give the strength to bear
    your infinite love's burden,
for him you strip away entire,
    once and for all, the curtain.

His sheltering home he shall not keep,
    his wealth too shall forsake him:
bringing him out onto the road
    a nobody you make him.
No honour now remains for him
    nor scorn nor shame nor fear –
possessed of you entire he sees
    the universal sphere.
So you stay in clear view, close,
    face to face with him,

and with your presence purely fill
    his spirit to the brim.
To his greed who knows such grace
    there's no end in view . . .
and yet he casts away all greed
    to make room for you.

67

Beautiful one, you came here at sunrise
with a *parijat*-flower sun-golden from the skies.
While still the town slept, none about their way,
a golden chariot took you away.
But as you passed my window there you paused
and inside shed the light of your sad eyes.
Beautiful one, you came here at sunrise.

Fragrance poured in as I dreamed.
The dark room quivered with joy, it seemed.
My *bina* silent in the dust
lay unassailed, yet uttered its sweet cries –

'Wake up, wake up, throw laziness aside',
again and again I thought, 'quick, rush outside!'
But when I woke up you had gone away.
It was our only meeting, I surmise . . .
beautiful one, you came here at sunrise.

68

When I used to play with you
   who you were no-one would know.
No fear or heart's dismay with you
   was mine in life's exuberant flow.
      To woods and fields all without end
      you called me, as my closest friend,
      and I laughed and ran my way with you
        dawn after dawn, so long ago.

Such songs you sang out clear and whole –
   whose meaning, dear one, none might chart.
Only with those songs sang my soul
   and danced my ever-exuberant heart.
      But what do I see now the play is done?
      A silent sky, hushed moon and sun,
      a universe poised still, apart,
        that at your feet keeps its eyes low.

69

Look, the boat is under way.
Who's to take your burdens, pray?
When you go ahead at last,
why not let the past stay past?
If you haul all on your back
on the shore alone you'll stay.

At the ferry as you stack
the burdens of the busy day,
always going and coming back,
the reason for it all has passed.

Call to the boatman, call him fast!
Now let the burdens float away . . .
and with a heart light in a new lack,
dedicate it to Him today.

70

Today somewhere in the clouds
   my mind has been mislaid.
Where has it gone running to?
   In what direction strayed?
      Over and over, its *bina* playing,
      lightning strikes where it is staying,
      while in my heart how dinningly
        the thunder's notes are played!

Clouds are lowering steadily,
embrace my body heavily,
until my soul is all engulfed
   in deep blue's darkest shade.

      A mad wind carried along in a dance
      becomes my friend in its crazy advance,
      hooting with laughter, hurtling where
        restraint is disobeyed.

71

Dear silent one if you are mute,
   words there need not be.
Overflowing with your silence
   my heart patiently
      I will support. As quiet as night
      that sets the unwinking stars alight,
      and still as her I will endure
         as her, submissively.

Morning will come will come will come –
   darkness all shall end.
In a shower-of-gold your Word
   sky-rending will descend.
      And from my birds' nests will a song
      rise in the syllables of your tongue?
      Will my woodland flowers break out
         to your melody?

72

As often as I light my lamp
    it goes out more and more.
So in my life your honoured place
    in dark is low and poor.
        From a plant that's withered at the root
        is the merest bud, no flowers shoot –
        so in my life your offering-gift
            is taken from pain's store.

Not even a speck is seen in me
    of glorious service, virtuous flame.
This your worshipper is here
    in the ragged clothes of shame.
        No-one is at his festival,
        no flute is playing, his home is dull.
        By weeping he has called you out
            to the broken temple door.

73

Your place from out the thick of all
    I shall remove –
yet for such worship in my home
    what room can serve?
Still I may keep you close and near,
if day and night you will appear
within the midst of all that's mine
    with generous love.

Such honour is not mine, indeed,
    that I may honour you,
and for your rites of worship make
    all preparation due.
Yet if in truth I love you, Lord –
then freely of its own accord
the flute will play, and flowers bloom
    to fill the grove.

74

Thunder sounds within your flute-song.
   No light pastoral
sweet notes awaken: but to this
     O make me sensible.
       Ease will not divert again:
       in my heart now I shall gain
       pure inspiration from the Life
        death makes invisible.

May the storm touch my mind with joy
    upon its *bina*-strings
of the seven seas that ten ways dance
    while your loud music sings.
       Now tear me from my comfort, take me
       to those depths, O dear one: make me
       know where in the restless surge
        peace lies all-powerful.

75

My being would bathe in the waters of
    your mercy's store.
Or in your presence how shall I
    bow down before?
        The grime is all too clear that clings
        to the basket of your offerings . . .
        myself at your feet I cannot
            set down therefore.

For so long as I carried on
    I felt no hurt,
although my body overall
    was smeared with dirt.
        Today in longing for that breast
        so pure, my heart weeps, weeps without rest –
        O do not let me lie in the dust,
            not any more.

76

When the great court is at an end
    shall I then sing a closing-song?
Perhaps before a Presence there
    all voiceless I shall gaze and long.
        The melody that's not yet played,
        will its song at last be made?
        Will love's pain in its golden note
            enter the dusk-air deep and strong?

For so long I have practised the tune
    day and night in my own heart.
If devotion's studious care
    in this life has played its part . . .
        upon the stream of a song-of-Earth
        I shall float the story of this birth,
        a lotus from the holy lake,
            to the Last Ocean carried along.

77

The pain the soul bears, and life's being
of pain, alas, even from birth's freeing –
  O let your flame tower high and higher,
  spare not, admit me to the fire
  though frail, all earth-bound pale desire
    into its ashes fleeing.

O sound the call, the call that must be,
  why needlessly postpone it?
This blind entanglement of the heart,
  tear it away, disown it!
    Now may the crash of thunder break –
    so let the noise your conch will make,
    pride-shattering, sleep-scattering, wake
      into a brilliant seeing.

78

When you call upon me to sing
    my heart is warmed by pride's embrace,
my two eyes water as I gaze
    unwaveringly upon your face;
and all that in me is hard-felt
in a song's nectar wants to melt;
and all my worship and soul's care
    wants to fly with a bird's free grace.

My love-song pleases, I can tell,
you like it well, you like it well:
and so because of it I dare
    to sit before you, take my place.

Though I may miss you with my heart,
I touch your feet by my song's art —
and call you friend, all unaware,
    enraptured in this singing space.

79

Let my love rush forward all at once
    Lord, and so be near, and so be near.
Let my deep hope all at once advance
    Lord, to where you hear, to where you hear.

At any place or moment that you call
let my mind at once reply; with all
obstruction levelled on the way between:
    Lord, you make it clear, you make it clear.

My beggar's plate out there that is so full
and rich in alms, let not a particle
be placed in it . . . while I am fed unseen
    Lord, with your gift dear, with your gift dear.

O my friend, O nearer One than all,
whatever in this life is beautiful,
today in your song singing, past all screen
    Lord, may it appear, may it appear.

80

They came to my house
    some time in the day.
They said, 'We will stay
    all out of the way.'
They said, 'Let us help
    serve God with our love –
and just what we find
    in the offering-tray,
when the worship is done
    and the crowd is all gone,
we will take for ourselves
    if we may.'

They came to my house
    frail-looking, unsure,
to stay in a corner
    in dirty clothes, poor.
At night then I saw
    them burst in, all bold
through my temple door,
    approach the store
of offerings-in-worship
    set down before –
and with dirty fingers
    steal them away.

81

They have stood in the road and uttered your name
    and charged a fee.
For money for that last fare from the *ghat*,
    there'll be none left, I see!
In the guise of being in your employ
wealth, life and all they take, destroy . . .
the little that I have to enjoy
    they plunder ruthlessly.

Today I see through their disguise,
    this falsely-dealing clique;
but they too see, alas, poor me
    as unresisting, weak.
Therefore all guile is cast away
and shame is lost to them. Today
they stand, head high, and block the way
    in front of me.

82

My soul has woken in night's moonlit heaven.
– O will the space around you offer haven?
   And shall I look upon that beautiful face?
   And will my longing heart gaze on that place?
   And circling round and about before your feet
      ever again, will my tear-songs be woven?

Boldly to raise myself to your foot's station
I have not dared, but stay in fear's position.
I am prostrate, pressing my face to the ground,
   afraid you may give back what may be given.

If you draw near and take me by the hand
and in that closeness call on me to stand –
then all the endless poverty of life
   will disappear, at the same moment even.

83

The promise was that in a boat together you and I,
    we two alone would drift, would drift without design;
and in the three worlds none would know about our
                          pilgrimage,
    what land it could be we were off to, up to which
                       coast-line.
        Adrift in the shoreless sea I'd sing
        a song just for your listening,
    as if a wave freed from the knot of words –
and with quiet laughter you would hear these singing notes
                    of mine.

Today isn't it time yet – is there still work to be done?
    O my dear the dusk is tumbling down over the shore,
and in the pale light over there all the seaside birds
    take wing, each one of them, to nests they left before.
        When will you come down to the *ghat*?
        When will the mooring-rope be cut?
    As if the last ray left the setting sun –
the boat will pierce the tracklessness of night and leave
                  no sign.

84

How to break clear of a closed room here!
    In the world's full ken
outside I shall take my place and ride
    life's chariot – when?
In a violent love I will swiftly move
here and there among all . . . at the market-stall
as in all I do, I will find with you
    our union then.
Outside I shall take my place and ride
    life's chariot – when?

In sorrow and joy brimming with hope
    and longing's dream,
I will dive into that wave-cascade
    and breast the stream.
You will hold me dear – and the truth I'll hear
of all the world's throng in their jabbering song –
as by good I am racked, by evil attacked
    again and again.
Outside I shall take my place and ride
    life's chariot – when?

85

Back to the blindness of a closed mind
    I will not go —
to sit in a corner of self-wit
    and nothing know.
Tying myself to you to embrace you
I scarcely hold you but replace you
with myself. I am caught in the knot
    of my own rope's throw.

Within the universe itself
    when you are found
Lord of my heart then my heart too
    will be your ground.
My mind is as a flower-stalk which
the lotus of the world makes rich . . .
upon it the full revelation
    may you show.

86

If you woke me, Lord, today,
    don't turn back now, don't turn back –
      bless me, look my way.
        Clouds of *Asharh*, storm-intense
        pour on forest-branches dense . . .
      while lazy night, as rain descends,
        in sleep will stay.
      Don't turn back now, don't turn back –
      bless me, look my way.

As lightning stabs incessantly
   and torrent-waters spring
the soul that is awake in me
   has a desire to sing.
        My heart, that would tears' water shed,
        searches the dark sky overhead –
        as one with his two arms outspread
          and anxious words to say.
        Don't turn back now, don't turn back –
        bless me, look my way.

87

O take me, tear me away,
    don't wait any more!
Let me not drop in the dust –
    pluck me before!
Whether your garland will show
this flower or not, I don't know –
but that your fortunate blow
    may come, I implore!
Tear me away, tear me away,
    don't wait any more!

When at the ruin of day
    night has come on –
the time of your rite will pass
    unseen, be gone.
What little I offer you,
while still in bloom, is due –
the fragrance, nectar and hue
    for your temple-store.
Tear me away, tear me away,
    don't wait any more!

88

You I want. Only you,
  dearest, I desire.
Let me always say this from
  the heart, no liar.
Other hopes of night and day
that lead me on, lead me astray;
for all are false. Only you,
  dearest, I desire.

As night's prayer-word is unheard
  that seeks sun's fire —
so dream-deluded, it is you,
  dearest, I desire.
As peace is shattered by storm's riot
and yet at heart that storm seeks quiet —
so injuring you, yet only you,
  dearest, I desire.

89

Mine is a bold love that would take
     no weak position;
and yet it weeps, because it is
     confused in vision.
Why does it sink down in sleep's flow,
in slack delights and beauty's show?
My love would wake with you and go
     on joy's mad mission!

When fearfully-costumed dancers' feet
fly to a demoniac beat —
in shame and fear some will retreat,
     dazed with suspicion.
Let my love welcome openly
that lovely violent one to me . . .
let petty heavens-of-hope all be
     sent to perdition!

90

Strike me more, I will endure it —
    let the blows come.
With a harder tune now make
    these life-strings thrum.
As yet the melody in them waking
is minor, its full tune not taking —
a crueller cadence, by your making,
    let it become.

Kind compassion, O my dear one
    is not the whole.
In tender music's play let me not
    lose my soul.
Let all fires explode and quiver,
let all winds cry out and shiver . . .
with all the skies awake, deliver
    the all and sum.

91

You have done well, cruel one,
   you have done this well.
Start the quick flames in my heart,
   let them rage and swell.
      If an incense-stick's not lit
      no sweet smell can pour from it.
      The lamp that's left in dark to sit
       has dark words to tell.

While in dark this mind of mine
   all unconscious lies,
the shocking blow that is your touch
   is its certain prize.
      When in shame and undiscerning
      blindness, from you I am turning –
      you thunderously, as if through burning
       transform my black hell.

92

Knowing that you are God, I keep my distance.
   I do not hold you close – but keep my place,
and touch your feet in a filial observance.
   I do not clasp your hands in a friend's embrace.
      Where you came down in simplest love, to show
      yourself to me as mine – I do not go
      and there, in loving joy as your companion,
         enfold you to me with a welcoming face.

A brother are you and a Lord among brothers.
But yet I do not look towards those others.
Why don't I share all that I have among them,
   and so your brother's hand with my wealth grace?
      But I am not before you. I do not enter
      the joy and grief of all; do not surrender
      my life unwearyingly in what I do.
         I do not dive into life's ocean-race.

93

In the works that you perform
   shall I not take some part too?
Won't you wake me with your power
   in this day of work to do?
      In bad-and-good and rise-and-fall,
      in breaking-and-building of the hall
      of all the world – allow me, loved one,
         standing beside you, to know you.

In some shadowy lonely place
   by the to-and-fro untainted
of busy time, in dusk's dark space,
   I thought we would be acquainted.
      Darkness, solitude . . . I seem
      to see a meeting in a dream.
      In your market-place now call me,
         in the buying-and-selling queue!

94

Where freely with the wide world you combine
our meeting is. Nothing of you is mine
    in any place that's set apart:
    not forest, nor in my own heart:
but where you are of all, O treasured one –
    there you are mine.

Where you spread out your arms with all to entwine –
there, only there, the love wakes that is mine.
    Love is not secret, shut away or far,
    but gives itself like light. And that you are
the wealth and joy of all, O treasured one –
    this joy is mine.

95

Call me now call me
into your tender cool and sacred
depths of darkness.

At every moment of the futile day
words in an infinite delirious play
tax the mind's powers as tired spent hours
    through the dust haul me.

Free me O free me
into your generous silent endless
deeps of darkness.

When in the soundless night all words have died,
let my outer shell mix in with the outside –
and in my inner wholeness may you see me
    and recall me.

96

Where the world claims its bounty, that rich hall —
how will my mind travel to it at all?
     In a glorious vessel stars and sun
     carry light on in a golden run,
and endless life across the heavens will fall.
How will my mind travel to it at all?

Where the throne of giving you instal,
how will my mind travel to it at all?
     Where each day you pour fresh and share
     the richness of yourself . . . from there
O in my life will there not be a call?
How will my mind travel to it at all?

97

You let a flower bloom in my song,
O my Lord, in your dear kindness.
Seeing it I am carried along
by joy. As if it might belong
to me, I offer it. Knowing I long
to give it in my childish blindness,
you take it in a laughing fondness,
my sense of honour not to wrong.

If later, when the worship-hours
are over and done, the song must weaken –
wither and droop and lose its powers
to dust – no injury is taken.
In the palm of your hand what endless showers
of wealth are tossed – are broken and shaken!
If for an instant my life flowers,
a soul is left for ever strong.

98

I shall go on turning, turning to you.
O may this one wish of my life hold true.
    Only gazing, only gazing,
     to a fixed place my thoughts raising,
     past all longing, all pain's crazing,
still intent, even in the work I do.

On every side new wishes run, stream through:
still let this one wish of my life hold true.
    Let it awake, night after night –
     with the ache of the One may it unite –
     on the thread of the One may it fasten tight
day by day, in a joyful singing too.

99

Asharh has come. The skies are overcast
again, the scent of rain is carried past
    upon the wind, and my old heart today
    thrills, as if a wild-beat tune to play,
        to see the new clouds come, so dense and vast.
        Asharh has come. The skies are overcast.

From time to time over the great terrain
on new grass falls the shadow of the rain.
    'It has come it has come' my heart is saying this,
    'it has come it has come' a song sings out in bliss.
        In my eyes in my heart it has come. Sudden and fast
        Asharh has come. The skies are overcast.

100

Monsoon weather now I see
    all around humanity.
In an angry muttering
    it has come here, cloaked and shrouded.
Rising in a sky dense-clouded,
    furious at heart it dances –
and a mass of cloud advances
    over-running its own bounds.
Clasped in a close union
    clouds fly on unfaltering.
Who can tell what drives them on?
    From that drift the thunder sounds.
Monsoon weather now I see
    all around humanity.

Into the far-distant regions
    cloud-accumulations go
in their companies and legions.
    What propels them they don't know,
nor when they dissolve and fall,
    as the *Srabon*-torrents come,
from a great hillside to the sea.
    Do they comprehend at all
what land that was? where it might be?
    How grand and splendid they become!

Yet it takes them unawares,
the terrible life and death that is theirs.
Monsoon weather now I see
all around humanity.

In that rumbling over there
in the havoc of the north-east,
where a storm takes on its nature,
what is whispered on the air?
What irrevocable future,
in the deepening shadows pieced
on the horizon, in night-stillness
carries its own speechless pain?
As it reaches to its fullness
in the dark skies of the brain,
black imagination leads
into what forthcoming deeds?
Monsoon weather now I see
all around humanity.

101

O my Lord, filling this being to the brim,
to sip at what sweet nectar it is your whim!
　　Poet, it is your pleasure to look at the light
　　of your world's picture by my eyes' sight;
　　and through my rapt hearing you listen in silence,
　　　　yourself intent to hear Creation's hymn.

This very Creation of yours, O Lord,
has written a singular wonderful word
　　in me. From that, and your love, springs
　　my song. And as your singer sings
　　you glimpse yourself with such pure sweetness –
　　　　making a gift of yourself in him.

102

This then is my longing, and no less,
that some grand song may your delight express:
    and though your sky will see how small my door,
    your loving stream of light may not withdraw –
        and that in me the six seasons may come dancing,
            simple in style, each day in different dress.

Let your delight be free and never find
resistance in my body or my mind.
    O in my depths of grief may that pure light
    awake, flame out, that is of your delight,
        my poor means cancelling, and so advancing
            in all I do . . . break through and flower and bless.

103

Towards a rendez-vous in the dark
      alone I go.
– But who is keeping pace with me?
      I do not know.
I dodge and circle round and turn
and try to lose him – still to learn
the pest is with me I thought left
      a while ago.

With his ghastly jumpiness
      the ground is quivering.
To every word that I may say
      he adds his gibbering.
O Lord, this fellow is my 'I' –
all sense of shame has passed him by.
With what shame will I meet you now
      with him in tow!

104

At all of you I gaze out, all the race.
Among the all allow me my own place.
    In dust, in with the lowest of the low,
        and where no payment's made for seating-space,
    no lines are drawn, and there's no mark to show
        some attribute of honour or disgrace –
            among the all allow me my own place.

Where there's no hiding-off from the outside,
    where in all nakedness I show my face,
where ownership is freely self-denied,
and where the truth of all this does not hide,
    even where I stand all poor and without trace
    of shame, His perfect gift I will embrace.
        Among the all allow me my own place.

105

No more under this deadweight 'I'
    is my head staying!
No more a beggar at his own door
    for alms is praying!
Before your feet my burden throwing,
I shall be free in a careless going –
no more of it for my ears' hearing
    or my lips' saying!
No more under this deadweight 'I'
    is my head staying!

In everything I yearn towards
    and seek to hold,
the light at once dies with my touch
    and it is cold.
O these two hands are so impure,
their gifts I too cannot endure.
Unless your love calls out – no more
    of heart's obeying!
No more under this deadweight 'I'
    is my head staying!

106

O my soul, awaken slowly
   in this holy pilgrims'-place,
where India's greatness reigns, before
    the ocean's space.
      I spread my arms here – I revere
        and worship God-in-man:
      his praise repeat, to joy's fierce beat,
        with all the heart I can.
      These thought-clad mountains, this field-ground
      with river-rosary-garlands wound,
      here each day always with your gaze
        the pure Earth you embrace,
      where India's greatness reigns, before
        the ocean's space.

No-one knows from where it flows
   or who set it in motion,
this wild flood-force of humanity's course,
    to mingle in mid-ocean.
      Here are Aryans and non-Aryans,
        Moguls, tribes-of-East,
      and Huns and Scythians, Pathans, Dravidians,
        all in a body pieced.
      Now the West has opened its door –
      and bringing gifts all through it they pour,

to give, to take, their mixed mixing make . . .
    their way they will not retrace,
where India's greatness reigns, before
    the ocean's space.

All in uproar, awash with war,
    and singing victory's song,
past desert-track, over mountain's back,
    they made their way along.
        And still all, all within me call,
            no-one is ever far,
        and still my blood remembers the thud
            of the different sounds of war.
        O *rudra-bina* play play play –
        those distant in their scorn today,
        their own door breaking and their way making –
            come, join us in this race,
        where India's greatness reigns, before
            the ocean's space.

Of old upon the heart-strings rolled
    Om in its great sound
unending where the One in prayer
    rose ringing all around.
        Through trial of austere self-denial,
            as various gifts were laid
        in the fire of the One – division was undone
            and one great spirit made.
        With that endeavour, that prayer today,

the door stands open where the holy flames play . . .
now let us here stand close and near
   with lowered face,
where India's greatness reigns, before
   the ocean's space.

In the holy fire-maze see now ablaze
   sorrow's blood-red flame.
As it burns in the heart, to bear it is our part —
   it is written beside our name.
      O my soul, bear your burden whole,
         the call of the One come to know,
      and your shame and fear will be conquered here,
         and your sense of injury go.
      After intolerable pain is borne —
      what a magnificent life will be born!
      The Mother wakes in her nest. Day breaks
         at the end of night's slow pace,
      where India's greatness reigns, before
         the ocean's space.

O come Aryans, come non-Aryans,
   Hindus, Muslims, all,
come all of you, you English too,
   come you of the Christian call.
      Come here Brahmin, but first determine
         to clean your mind and so
      hold the hand of all. Come you who fall,
         let the great insult go.

Come come quickly where the Mother is crowned,
to this pilgrims'-place where the pots are found
that are not yet full of the touched-by-all-
   -made-holy-water-of-grace,
where India's greatness reigns, before
   the ocean's space.

107

Among the meanest your feet go,
    where all the destitute are tossed,
        among the least, among the low,
          among the lost.
To touch your feet, in my heart's love,
I bow – but my heart does not move.
Where your feet, suffering insult, go,
    there my heart's reverence has not crossed,
        among the least, among the low,
          among the lost.

Pride is denied your to-and-fro
    in ragged clothes of cheapest cost,
        among the least, among the low,
          among the lost.
Where wealth and dignity abound
I hope your friendship will be found.
But friendless homes that friendship know –
    there, where my heart has not crossed –
        among the least, among the low,
          among the lost.

108

O my unfortunate land, for all those you shame,
the insult you endure shall be the same.
    For all you betray,
    rights taking away,
distancing from your warmth, denying their claim,
the insult you endure shall be the same.

From human contact holding yourself apart,
you stand aloof from the Lord of the human heart.
    When in God's wild anger
    comes famine-hunger,
to eke out your food with all must be your aim.
The insult you endure shall be the same.

When you dismiss from your throne in bullying style,
you carelessly thrust your own power into exile.
    Ground under heel
    with those you must reel
in the dust, there is no other way but to feel the blame.
The insult you endure shall be the same.

If you fling one down, he will have you tied and bound.
If you keep one back, he will drag you along the ground.
    If you cover and cloak
    in ignorance dark –
he will hide your good, its terrible distance frame.
The insult you endure shall be the same.

Ten thousand years since the burden of scorn began.
Still you ignore the god that is God-in-Man.
    Can't you look down, see
    where in the dust He
came down — and the god of Untouchables became?
The insult you endure must be the same.

You can't see the messenger of death standing outside.
You can't see his curse etched in the nation's self-pride.
    If you still won't call
    from the heart to all,
but all-apart, knot yourself to your pride's name —
in death's ash then endure with all the same.

109

Don't let go, hold on tight,
   and win through, my dear.
All night's darkness is in flight.
   Gone is all your fear.
Look above – on the East's face,
over the deepest forest-place,
the morning star has risen clear.
   Gone is all your fear.

These are marauders of the night:
   self-doubt, the sceptic's sneer,
dejection, sloth. At dawn's light
   see them disappear.
Come outside, come quickly, fly –
look up, look up and see – the sky
is full of light and bright and sheer.
   Gone is all your fear.

110

My heart is full, my heart is full –
   now what you wish for me, prepare.
Within you are all-powerful –
   then rob me of my outward share.
      My life-fulfilment if you send
      where all thirst has found an end,
      then on a blazing desert-track
        let the sun magnify its glare.

This game you play with such disguise –
   I love it too, to play my part.
For when with tears you fill my eyes,
   you also send a laughing heart.
      To loss of all I am resigned . . .
      and in a deep way all I find.
      From a warm lap you fling me far,
        to draw me back to your heart's care.

III

Can my speech utter that name? I say the word –
    and you know this, who know me – not in pride.
Yet when I say your name and some have heard
    my voice pronounce it – they mock and deride.
        O let me always keep in view
        that I live far away from you;
for when I feel my own stance is not true
    in my love-songs – for shame my heart has died.

O save me from the lie of arrogance,
    and keep me where my place is. When I see
all round me stare – remove me from that glance.
    O grant that your own eyes look down on me.
        If for your gifts I utter prayer,
        then let my song be heard nowhere.
I call you always as through dusty air,
    with my faults ever-fresh on every side.

112

When death comes to take your hand,
      who says all your goods shall stay?
All you have in life amassed,
      all in death you take away.
   When the gathering has ended,
   will you then leave empty-handed?
   What is yours is for your taking:
      take it finely on your way.

What a vast assortment of dross
      you have piled up on and on!
To be saved, then, at your going –
      let that be destroyed, be gone.
   I have come to this world-place
   to prepare myself for a space . . .
   let's go, royally-clothed and smiling,
      past death to the festival-play.

113

Today it seems a river streams
  of *Asharh*'s dawn.
Take, take it in till deep within
  the heart it's drawn.
Green, gold, blue together seen –
the nectar-light spread in between –
now in the sky far-reaching, keen
  a Word is born.
Take, take it in till deep within
  the heart it's drawn.

Walking the world's way as you go
  upon the land,
accept the flowers that you see grow
  on either hand.
And day and night, with those you find,
weave a garland for the mind,
that will of your good luck remind
  both eve and morn.
Take, take it in till deep within
  the heart it's drawn.

114

When Death at last at day's end makes his way
          towards your door,
what riches will you give him on that day?
          My life's full store
          laying out before,
an empty farewell then I shall not say –
when Death at last to my door makes his way.

    So many autumn and spring nights,
      so many dusk and dawn delights,
so many feelings fill life's cup with rain –
      so many fruits, so many flowers
      touch my heart with all the hours
of joy and sorrow, light and shade again.

      What riches I
      have gained thereby,
on that last day I shall to him display –
when Death at last to my door makes his way.

115

By your own wish and generous thought
made small, to this mean dwelling you resort;
and that sweet richness that within you lies
    dispels the hunger of my eyes.
On land and sea, in this and that disguise,
        you let yourself be caught.

Friend, father, mother you become –
and so made small, into my heart you come.
But do I by my own act make him less,
    the Lord of the World – in littleness
discover him and so to others confess,
        delivering false report?

116

The consummation of this life,
     the fullness that will be
death, my death – O my death
       speak now, speak to me.
    All my life is for your sake:
     for you each day I am awake;
     for you alone I bear the ache
       of joy, grief's agony.
    Death, my death – O my death
       speak now, speak to me.

All I am, all I have gained
     and all I hope for too,
and all my heart's love itself runs
      unknowingly to you.
    And all in you is unified
     in that dear glance of groom and bride,
     as life itself becomes a wife
      ever-devotedly.
    Death, my death – O my death
      speak now, speak to me.

In my heart a woven garland
     waits in readiness.
When will you appear, all-silent,
     smiling, in groom's dress?

Then no dwelling will there be,
no family, non-family . . .
but only in the lonely night
    a bride's true unity.
Death, my death – O my death
    speak now, speak to me.

117

A journeyer am I.
O who is there to hold me back? A lie
   is all this clinging knot of joy and pain . . .
   what we construct will far behind remain.
   As for the dead weight of material gain,
     scattered and torn to pieces it will lie.

A journeyer am I.
I sing a song on the way and my heart is high.
   My body's fort will all defenceless be,
   from the shackles of desire I shall be free –
   beyond all good and bad the way takes me,
     as from this world to that one I pass by.

A journeyer am I.
The load I bear – all that from me will fly.
   The sky's call to its far ways I have heard
   in a song of the unknown that has no word.
   O whose flute is it that my soul has stirred
     at dusk and dawn with penetrating cry?

A journeyer am I.
I do not know which early day's dark sky
   it was I came out into. Then no song
   of bird was heard; nor did I know how long
   the night would stay. But on the dark lay strong
     a seeing gaze, not to flicker or die.

A journeyer am I.
In the last dusk what home will I descry?
O what star there its lit lamp keeps?
What wind with what flower's fragrance weeps?
And who is it, in time that never sleeps,
who looks upon me there with tender eye?

118

See on the chariot that drives through the air –
out on the way, flag flying, He is there.
    You inside, in a corner installed –
    come out running, the rope's to be hauled,
    fall to it, join in, dive in the crowd –
        somehow, anyhow, grab your rope's share.

Your daily tasks keep you occupied? –
put these excuses all to the side.
    Abandon the petty rigmarole
    life fools you with. With body and soul
    pull, pull, pull in the dark and the light –
        village town forest hill everywhere.

Those wheels over there whirling around,
within don't you hear that glorious sound?
    Doesn't your life-blood ring loud and strong?
    Doesn't your heart drown death in its song?
    Surging to the tremendous future,
        don't your quick hopes rush out and dare?

119

Praise-song, prayer, devout prostration —
    all of this forget.
Why are you stationed in the temple,
    behind its closed door set?
Alone in darkness, hidden away —
to whom in secret do you pray?
Open your eyes, look, look about —
    God is not here yet.

He has gone to break the ground
    that the farmer breaks —
or breaking stones with that one who
    year through, a new road makes.
In downpour, sun's glare, with them all
He lets the dust on His hands fall.
Like Him, your spotless clothes throw out —
    let the earth's dust be met.

You seek salvation? Where will you look?
    Where is salvation found?
The Lord, self-linked with all, must be
    to the mass of people bound.
Forget the flowers, the meditation:
you will find true purification
in soiled, torn clothes, when most devout —
    when you pour with sweat.

120

Boundless one and bounded, you play a tune of your own.
With you in my heart all sweetness there is shown.
All the hues and scents and songs, every rhythm that
                                        belongs,
wake my heart to beauty's form, O you of form unknown.
With you in my heart heart's loveliness is known.

When you are one with me then all is open in the world.
The ocean of the cosmos plays and back and forth is
                                        swirled.
And in my own tears' water flows a light that too much
                                        beauty knows –
your light that casts its shape in me where yet no shadow's
                                        thrown.
With you in my heart heart's loveliness is known.

121

And so your joy has entered me –
   and you yourself have come down too.
Without me, Lord of the three worlds,
   this love of yours would be untrue.
     With me you have opened a fair,
     a play of emotions everywhere,
     as your desires all differently
       wave-surge in me through and through.

So you, installed as king of kings,
   still go about for my heart's sake,
in such heart-captivating ways,
   now here, now there, always awake.
     And your love, too, is here to see
     in the love of the devotee:
     and there, in two-fold unity,
       your form is clear and in full view.

122

The bed of comfort, honour's chair —
    friends, you may avoid.
Then taking leave of all, we shall,
    more happily employed,
set out with one intent and so
together to the outside go:
and journey to the home of the low,
    where honour's null and void.

Our blame shall be our ornament,
    our necklace all of thorn;
and our heads, too, will know the weight
    of slander and of scorn.
And where, at grief's last home, we stop
and in that dust our heads we stoop —
renunciation's empty cup
    we fill up, overjoyed.

123

The day you band of heroes left
  the home of the Lord,
where was that tremendous strength
  secretly stored?
Where were your weapons? Armour where?
Poor weak defenceless without care —
from all sides on you everywhere
  blows rained and poured,
the day you band of heroes left
  the home of the Lord.

The day you band of heroes came
  to the home of the Lord,
again where was the tremendous strength
  secretly stored?
Bows arrows swords had been let drop,
the smile of peace had opened up —
and life's rich overflowing cup
  was your reward,
the day you band of heroes came
  to the home of the Lord.

124

I thought in my mind, at the end of the day
my journey would cease with nowhere to stay.
    Maybe no path, or no more to do,
      or rations at last would give out. And I knew
      (I thought) that I would go into hiding,
        in torn dirty clothes, my life in decay.

Yet look today at this endless sweet play,
this freshness — what is it? — within holding sway.
    When words are weary and all's spoken,
    a new song's murmuring is awoken.
    Where an old path leads into an ending,
      to a new land you have opened the way.

125

This my song has cast off now
    all ornament and frill:
proud apparel, in your presence,
    it must not wear still.
Trinket-jinglings fall between
our time-of-closeness, like a screen . . .
and all you say to me is lost
    in that loud thrill.

Merely futile, in your presence,
    is my poet's conceit.
O Poet, may I be held back,
    and set down at your feet!
If with a sure care for life's state,
the flute is straight that I create —
then all of its air-openings
    your melody will fill.

126

In humiliation's sorrow,
    under insult's shriek –
where is the impoverishment?
      How does it make me weak?
        When cast upon the dusty ground,
        no need then for a chair to be found.
        From there unhesitatingly
          your blessing I will seek.

When I hear fine words instead
    and with pleasure I glow,
that something spurious has been said
    in my heart I know.
      I take that praise and set it out
      to look well as I go about . . .
      and shall I then go visiting you?
        – No time, so to speak.

127

The child you clothe as in a monarch's dress,
   and give a necklace all of jewels to wear –
what games and sports are his? What happiness?
    How heavy all the richness he must bear!
     In case the robes tear, or are soiled
     by dust's mark, or are creased and spoiled –
he must stay far apart. Great cares oppress
   his anxious mind when he moves anywhere,
the child you clothe as in a monarch's dress,
   and give a necklace all of jewels to wear.

'These kingly clothes, mother – what are they for?
   For what, this jewelled necklace that I wear?
O I shall rush outside if you open the door,
    in the sun and the mud and the dust and the wind's air!'
     A world of people at their play
     sing out in festival all day
a song that echoes in its thousandness
   all round – but he has no right to be there,
the child you clothe as in a monarch's dress,
   and give a necklace all of jewels to wear.

128

Two strings, a thick one with a fine,
       are twisted, caught:
and so life's *bina* does not play
       the tune it ought.
    In the harsh discordant strain
    my heart has given up in pain
    as suddenly, again and again,
       my song stops short.
Alas! life's *bina* does not play
       the tune it ought.

Such distress has come of this
       I cannot bear it,
but journey to your court in shame
       with a dead spirit.
    Among your virtuosi band
    I may not stay, near those tunes grand –
    but at the back of all I'll stand
       in the outer court.
Alas! life's *bina* does not play
       the tune it ought.

129

Songs fit only to ignore,
gifts on which to set no store –
    it seems no gift is fully made,
    it seems a trick on you I've played.
    When will the worship due be paid
        that life, once whole, need pay no more?

The service that for others I do –
    filling the offering-plate over and over –
is the false all dressed up with the true,
    in case my poverty they discover.
        Yet from you what can be concealed?
        Then let a bold gift be revealed:
        all that I have, to you I yield,
            this soul, all undisguised and poor.

130

In me your own sweet life-game has its play,
and that is why on Earth I have my day.
    The door will open wide that was shut tight,
    and my proud ego will be put to flight.
    Within your world-existence of delight,
        of me, of mine – nothing at all will stay.

Life rescues me as death takes me away:
in me your own sweet life-game has its play.
    All wishes will be finished that were mine,
    being re-defined in your one love so fine.
    In joy-and-sorrow's living rich design,
        apart from you – nothing at all will stay.

131

What brings this nightmare on, to make
    such chaos out of life, such ill?
I see, when weeping I awake,
     my mother's lap protects me still.
        I had thought someone else was here
        and so I shook and fought in fear –
        but as I see your smile I know
           you hold me, rock me at your will.

Life itself gives such a shaking,
    its fears and sorrows and joys that fall,
that nothing else is for the taking
    it seems – but that must be my all.
        This dark haze from my eyes is torn
        in the instant of the light of dawn –
        as to fulfilment all waves flow
           towards you, reaching, and are still.

132

I search for you in songs — my heart
    roams far and free
each single day that comes to be.
    I enter, my songs going before,
    home after home through door after door,
        and with them go as they go here and there
        caressingly.

So much they have let me know,
so many hidden paths they show,
    so many stars in the sky of the heart
    they have let me see.

      When mystery's realm is crossed at last
      and the land of sorrow and joy is past,
        to what great home in the evening dusk
        will they bring me?

133

My search for you is never done,
even when my life ends in dawn's sun.
    I shall enter a new world's being,
    my sight awakened to a new seeing –
    and I shall wear, in this light's freeing,
        your new thread, joining as in one.
            My search for you is never done.

What end, what end can be for you?
Your game is played forever new.
    I do not know or understand
    in what attire, Lord, you will stand
    and smiling, come to take my hand –
        my life by a new love overrun.
            My search for you is never done.

134

Let all song-forms as one their melodies move.
O let my last song celebrate my love!
    With that joy where the laughing earth
    brings grass and tree to restless birth –
    and that mad duo, life and death,
    spin round the planet in their groove –
O let my last song celebrate my love!

With that uproarious joy that takes the form –
and wakes the sleeping world up – of a storm;
    and with that joy of sorrow's tears
    in which the lotus of pain appears;
    and that joy that leaves all to dust –
    for which what words can speak enough? –
O let my last song celebrate my love!

135

Imprisoned in your knot I know
    that I shall never now be free;
I know too, when you cast me low,
    that upright now I shall not be.
        Then you untie me, let me go,
        and help me stand; and then I know
        that in your arms I'm shaken so –
            your arms that rock me ceaselessly.

With fear you wake me if I drowse,
yet from a nightmare's fear you rouse.
        You call me and yourself you show,
        and then hide, where I do not know,
        yet I know I have lost you though . . .
            but from where are you answering me?

136

When your state is as a child's,
    weak and insecure,
in your inner heart of hearts
    so may it endure.
        When a soft blow overturns you,
        falling dust in mud-filth churns you,
        or a light flame-flicker burns you
            fearfully, past cure –
        in your inner heart of hearts
            so may it endure.

When your life-power comes and all
    is vital and awake,
and His nectar full-of-fire
    is the drink you take –
        O run outside, don't hesitate,
        no dust can spoil your spotless state,
        the chains you wear are without weight
            as you go free and sure.
        In your inner heart of hearts
            so may it endure.

137

That I shall be yours with a heart
        eternal-true –
O Truth, when may that fortunate day
        to me fall due?
'Truth truth truth' is my lips' prayer,
my mind is wholly in truth's care,
so at the worldly limit, there
        I will pass through.
O Truth, when may your full display
        be brought to view?

Staying apart from you I die
        by untruth's hand.
Where is the sense in being here,
        in this ghosts' land?
My 'I' self-cleansing, self-effacing
is lost in you, by your displacing . . .
at last if true to you my life
        is rescued new.
O Truth, when will my death itself
        find death in you?

138

O Lord, even as your mastery I discover –
still let this scrap of self, my 'I', stay over.
Now as I witness you on every side,
and with that One-in-All am unified,
and day and night your loving praise provide,
still let this self of foolish wants stay over –
O Lord, even as your mastery I discover.

Nowhere can my 'I' hide you or cover –
then let a scrap of self, no more, stay over.
This life is yielded up to that sweet play
of yours, for which you hold me here today;
and as I stay, bound close, in your arms' sway –
the merest knots that tie, let them stay over –
O Lord, even as your mastery I discover.

139

Your gifts enrich me to the highest degree.
If I die now I will die happily.
How many tunes, day and night, you bring
into my heart! What joy, what grief they sing!
O in such guises you come entering
my house with your enchanting sorcery!
If I die now I will die happily.

That I have not received you properly
I know: nor is my life all it should be.
That all is my good fortune, this I know;
I recognise the touch that you bestow;
and what you are, I know this well: and so
the raft of my faith floats, supporting me.
If I die now I will die happily.

140

O boatman on the voyage-from-birth,
    with the boat's helm in your care,
can you hear rise distantly,
    from the far shore, the flute's air?
O will the boat, deep in day's age,
touch ground at the landing-stage?
Is there an array of lamps
    in dusk's darkness shining there?

As if upon my mind it played,
from that far shore, in evening's shade,
whose smile across the sea has come,
    floating on the cool clear air?

At journey's start, in day's first hours,
I had picked and brought some flowers.
Now take the freshest of them here,
    and the flower-baskets prepare.

141

All my body, all my mind
I would at a stroke relinquish –
this black shadow leave behind.
Let that fire its shape abolish,
in that ocean let it vanish,
at those feet O may it perish,
    this delusion blind –
    all my body, all my mind.

When I see it occupy
a space, O Lord, for shame I die.
This shadow-mark of deepest dark,
    O take, cast far behind –
    all my body, all my mind.

In my heart what screen can be?
One and in entirety
will you appear when once you clear
    this delusion blind –
    all my body, all my mind.

142

At the day of going this is the word
    that I would first declare:
all I have seen, all that has been
    my own, is past compare.
        Where light's ocean its wave propels,
        the hundred-petalled lotus swells . . .
        that nectar rich was mine, for which
            a thankful heart I bear.
        At the day of going this is the word
        that with the world I'd share.

So much I played, so much I saw
    within this house of play,
as from the universal forms
    such beauty came my way.
        And that touch, too, my body knew
        of His form that no form can view . . .
        if now an ending He'll allow,
            so let an end be there.
        At the day of going this is the word
        that with the world I'd share.

143

My name conceals. To occupy
its prison-dungeon is to die.
 Forgetting all, I prettify
 my name, I wreathe it in the sky . . .
  still in the darkness is let lie
  the truth. And that is lost thereby.

With dust on dust I glorify
this name of mine, exalt it high.
 My mind will work non-stop to try
 and keep it pure, all fault deny –
  such care I lavish on this lie,
  my name. And all is lost thereby.

144

When you erase my name, O Lord,
 then I shall be set free that day;
and rescued from its self-made dream
 my life, re-born, in you will stay.
  But then I write my name's design,
  obliterating your words' line.
  This catastrophic life of mine –
   how long shall I endure it, pray?

My name steals everybody's clothes,
 intent upon its own parade;
and drowns out everybody's tune,
 intent on its own serenade.
  This name of mine – let it be gone!
  Your name my name shall rest upon:
  and so with all I will be one,
   without a name to pave the way.

145

Something obstructs me, and I would
    escape, but weep pain's tear.
I go to you to ask for aid –
    but die of shame when near.
        O you are my life's jewel, past measure:
        apart from you, what other treasure?
        Yet my room's filled with lumber which
            I cannot seem to clear.

It hides the heart, drowns you in dust,
    such life is buried here . . .
I hate the clutter for all I'm worth,
    and yet I hold it dear.
        So much undone, so much deceit,
        such failure, so much 'staying-discreet' –
        I ask you for my blessing but
            my heart is blocked by fear.

146

If then for your kindness
    I do not ask you, Lord,
still in kindness draw me
    your sacredness toward.
        The artificial treasure
        that in forgetful leisure
            I blindly have adored,
                the flowers and fruits of pleasure . . .
        from this dust-play-place take me.
        Do not in scorn forsake me,
            but in your kindness wake me
                with fire's thrusting sword.

Truth's a bud, closed up
    within a contradiction.
Who apart from you
    unfurls its leaf's constriction?
        By your nectar's sending
        in deathless streams descending,
            death's pierced – and all's restored
                where want had been unending.
        In fortune's sad reversal
        true sense makes an arrival:
            in conflict's din and quarrel
                is your far-reaching Word.

147

Life's honouring-deeds we start and do not do —
I know, I know that these are counted too.
    The flowers that do not come to flower
    but drop to earth and lose their power,
the rivers that run dry in desert, never to renew,
I know, I know that these are counted too.

Today's intentions that are not seen through,
I know, I know that these are not untrue.
    All my deeds so long delayed,
    all the tunes I have not played
sound out on your *bina*'s strings, all performed by you.
I know, I know that these are counted too.

148

With one humble greeting, Lord,
    with one reverent bow,
that I may here in lowliness
    be near, may you allow.
As a *Srabon*-cloud aloft
burden-rich descends rain-soft —
    with one humble greeting, Lord,
       with one reverent bow,
     my heart before your palace door,
       let it lie now.

The many tunes flowing into one,
as all streams on, my own self gone —
    with one humble greeting, Lord,
       with one reverent bow,
     my song all free in the silent sea,
       let it die now.

As the swan seeks the holy lake
and day and night no rest will take —
    with one humble greeting, Lord,
       with one reverent bow,
     my soul alone on past death's throne,
       let it fly now.

149

What in life has always been
    a hint, not on display,
that which has never come to flower
    in the fresh light of day –
        in a gift I bring,
        in a song I sing
            at life's end, Lord, before you now
              and offer it today, –
            that which has never come to flower
            in the fresh light of day.

What may not finally be said,
    tied down in shape of word,
nor finds its phrasing in a song,
    the right notes never heard –
        how secretly
        for none to see
            in lovely youthful forms, O Friend
              it hides itself away, –
            that which indeed has never flowered
            in the fresh light of day.

From land to land as I go on
    it travels by my side.
Whatever's built or broken has
    that in its midst inside.
      In all it waits,
      all actions, states;
        in sleeping and waking it remains;
          yet all alone will stay, –
        that which indeed has never flowered
          in the fresh light of day.

To find it such a multitude
    for such an age has yearned;
who always from the outer door
    with empty hands returned.
      O who can see
      it cannot be:
        that all that hope of knowing you
          beneath its own sky lay, –
        that which indeed has never flowered
          in the fresh light of day.

150

This always-being-at-odds with you
    I won't abide!
Each day, it seems, my debt to you
    is multiplied.
All others, their respects to show,
in courtly garments come and go;
I lurk about, dressed mean and low,
    undignified.

How to express this pain-of-mind!
My heart is speechless and can find
no word, when near you, to be heard.
    I stay tongue-tied.

Don't turn me back; but set me free
of this scorned feeling. So let me
your bond-slave be: and at your feet
    at last reside.

151

I will give myself to the hands of love
   and I await its claim.
Later and later is the hour,
    I more and more to blame.
      To law's tight knots I have been led,
      to fixed decrees – and I have fled,
      content to undergo instead
        the punishment that came.
      I will give myself to the hands of love
      and I await its claim.

People's scorn, their mocking stare –
   it is all merited.
From the lowest depths I bear
   the shame heaped on my head.
      But now it is the end of day:
      the market fair is done; and they
      have in their anger gone away
        who came to call my name.
      I will give myself to the hands of love
      and I await its claim.

152

Apart from you, whoever else
    in the world loves me,
in a narrow shackling bond
    denies my liberty.
        Your love is greater than all, and so
        there is no binding in its flow:
        all hiddenly, without a sign,
            you keep your servant free.

All others, fearing I forget,
    will not let me alone:
and so it comes, day after day,
    no sight of you is shown.
        I may call you, I may not call –
        my happiness still is my all.
        Your happiness is to hope for mine,
            and only that to see.

153

Love's envoy, Lord, when will you send?
O then all my dispute will end.
    All else who come to see me start
    to threaten, dominate. My heart
        cries war: I turn them back: the door
          against all enemies I defend.

When he arrives all doors fly open,
when he arrives all bonds are broken,
    and I must answer to his call –
        then who will hold me, keep me penned?

He makes his solitary way,
and at his neck twined flowers sway.
    And now my heart will silent stay,
        as I become the garland's friend.

154

Because of you I sang my song,
    because of your deceit,
who gave so much to grieve, alas!
     and so much that was sweet.
        You offer yourself for capture – flee –
        approach – at once escape from me –
           and life's most sorrowing instant
            you constantly repeat.
        Because of this I sang my song,
          because of your deceit.

You tune your *bina* to a pitch
    so sharp and so acute,
my life is pierced all through – which you
     take up and play, your flute.
        In the sweet run of your tune's flight
        if time has found its end-of-night,
           O let me then be silent
            and set me at your feet.
        Life-long it was I sang my song
          because of your deceit.

155

I feel the ending is right here —
    where then does it lie?
Again an order issues forth
    from your court on high.
        To a new singing, a new song
        my heart wakes: as I go along,
            the drift of the new melody
            I cannot descry.

When with dusk's gold radiance
    all the tune is one;
when with the last evening-song
    all my singing's done —
        in the deep note of dead-of-night
        again life fills and floods with light . . .
            and not a hint of drowsiness
            will linger in the eye.

156

'What has no end is in the end' –
    this very sentence
at song's end sings within the mind
      at countless moments.
          The tune its last note may have met:
          as if it never could forget,
          the melody will play on yet
             into the silence.

When from the *bina*'s strings are struck
    notes all-insistent,
the greatest song of all is that
      which is far distant.
          The *bina*'s put by: that descends
          upon it then, its own tune lends . . .
          as when, the day at rest, dusk sends
             its own deep cadence.

157

If the day goes, if birds will no more sing,
    and if the wind is spent and no more blows,
then dear one, bring that deepest covering,
      and in the all-dense darkness me enclose . . .
        as when the Earth with dreams around
        is secretly and slowly wound;
           the lotus settles in night's offering;
             and as, eyes entering sleep, you cover those.

The one who travels down the road of scorn,
    whose strength, with his provisions, is exhausted;
the one whose clothes are soiled with dust and torn,
      who all too clearly shows how far he's worsted —
        let his keen wounds covered be
        in your kind deep secrecy . . .
           and boldly flowering now at the new dawn,
             let him be cooled where the dark nectar flows.

NOTES

THE FEW WORDS I have italicised carry more than the brief explanations offered below. Daily practical use, a tale of the gods, a historical occasion here and there add a significance, an intimacy scarcely to be conveyed in a footnote however long. In a less definable way the same may be said of the text as a whole. The familiar understanding, the touch of the very place from which a poem has originated, a translator can do no more than persuade towards: the language is there and the place is there, to be visited it may be at the least. So one hopes Rabindranath's own words will find a wider audience.

A religious practice needs mention as several poems assume an awareness of it. The offering of food to the deity is an essential part of Hindu worship. When (with priest's intervention) it is accepted by God it becomes *prashaad*, to be shared among the community. Other aspects of daily life that illuminate the text from within, so to speak, are more in the nature of a single act than a process, and a hint of the picture is clear. To enlarge the picture with apparatus outside the text may not be apt. In general there is a reason here to keep commentary down. Prosaic explanation runs the risk of diverting from a poem's intent (that is in the hands of neither original author nor translator). Perhaps it is better to err on the side of non-interference. Whatever for a cultural reason is unfamiliar, one hopes the poetry itself will make less distant, that has its own way of 'making the unknown known'.

Asharh	A month of the Bengali calendar: mid-June to mid-July (monsoon).
bina	A traditional stringed instrument (also played by Saraswati, goddess of learning and music). Often used by Tagore with a sense of the divine harmony

	attaching to a natural phenomenon: its 'music' and something more.
chokha-chokhi	Small river birds often seen in pairs.
ghat	Steps leading down to a river; a boarding-place or a landing-place.
juthi	A white flower of the monsoon renowned for its scent.
kash	A tall white flower of autumn.
malati	A white creeper-flower of the monsoon.
neepo	A tree with white-yellow circular flowers in the monsoon.
Om	The All. The holiest of sounds, containing in itself all sounds including silence, whose intonation is said to unite with the intonation pervading the universe.
parijat	A flower that blooms only in paradise.
Phalgun	Mid-February to mid-March (spring).
rakhi	-knot, -thread. A red thread with a cotton or silk flower tied round a brother's wrist by a sister on a special day. Tagore took the custom from West India and extended it to a ritual symbolising protective love between any two people.
rudra-bina	Smaller than the *bina* and of deeper tone. Its name suggests the awesome aspect of Shiva, the god who destroys all that must end. It is as if the instrument is accompanying Shiva in full freedom in his role as Nataraj, king of dancers.
sephali	A tree that blossoms in autumn with small white flowers with an orange stem.
shaal	A great forest-tree.
sitar	A traditional stringed instrument of lighter tone than the *bina*.
siuli	Another name for *sephali*.
Srabon	Mid-July to mid-August (monsoon).

APPENDIX

TAGORE published other collections of his free translations of his verse. A further twelve *Gitanjali* poems found their way into some of these. His English versions of the individual poems of the text number sixty-five in all and appear as follows:

G = English *Gitanjali* (London, The India Society, 1912)
TG = *The Gardener* (London, Macmillan & Co., 1913)
F = *Fruit-Gathering* (London, Macmillan & Co., 1916)
C = *Crossing* (London, Macmillan & Co., 1918)
P = *Poems* (Calcutta, Visvabharati, 1942; posthumous)

2	14 G	44	16 G	107	10 G
3	63 G	46	47 P	114	90 G
4	79 F	47	100 G	116	91 G
8	84 TG	56	49 G	119	11 G
10	83 G	57	4 C	121	56 G
16	18 G	58	39 G	123	85 G
17	27 G	61	26 G	124	37 G
18	22 G	62	45 G	125	7 G
20	23 G	68	97 G	127	8 G
22	3 G	71	19 G	132	101 G
24	79 G	78	2 G	134	58 G
25	84 G	80	33 G	138	34 G
26	74 G	83	42 G	142	96 G
28	11 C	87	6 G	143	29 G
30	59 G	88	38 G	145	28 G
31	15 G	91	6 C	147	18 C
34	46 G	92	77 G	148	103 G
35	28 C	97	65 C	149	66 G
36	70 G	99	48 P	151	17 G
37	44 C	101	65 G	152	32 G
38	46 C	103	30 G	157	24 G
39	13 G	105	9 G		

About the Translator

Joe Winter (born in London, 1943) began to write poetry at the age of nineteen. He taught English in secondary schools in London from 1967 to 1994, and on taking early retirement moved to Calcutta to live and write. His collected poems have been published in a series of 16 volumes by Writers Workshop in Calcutta. Previous translations of his include the Middle English poem 'Pearl' in a modern version. Many of his articles on literary and other topics have appeared in *The Statesman* of Calcutta. At present he is working on a collection of translations of the poems of Jibanananda Das, as well as on further translations of Tagore. He has recently completed a sequence of 50 sonnets entitled 'Guest and Host' arising from his experience of living in India.

Some classic translations from Anvil

Borrowed Ware
MEDIEVAL PERSIAN EPIGRAMS
Translated by Dick Davis

DANTE
The Divine Comedy
Translated by Peter Dale

GOETHE
Roman Elegies and other poems
Translated by Michael Hamburger

JULES LAFORGUE
Poems
Translated by Peter Dale

The Selected Poems of Li Po
Translated by David Hinton

ARTHUR RIMBAUD
A Season in Hell
and other poems
Translated by Norman Cameron

Sappho Through English Poetry
Edited by Peter Jay and Caroline Lewis

The Song of Songs
Translated by Peter Jay

FRANÇOIS VILLON
Poems
Translated by Peter Dale

Modern and contemporary translations

BEI DAO
Landscape Over Zero
Translated by David Hinton with Yanbing Chen

NINA CASSIAN
Life Sentence
Edited by William Jay Smith

NIKOS GATSOS
Amorgos
Translated by Sally Purcell

NIKOLAY GUMILYOV
The Pillar of Fire
Translated by Richard McKane

IVAN V LALIĆ
A Rusty Needle
Fading Contact
Translated by Francis R Jones

FEDERICO GARCÍA LORCA
A Season in Granada
Edited and translated by Christopher Maurer

VASKO POPA
Collected Poems
Translated by Anne Pennington and Francis R Jones

GEORGE SEFERIS
Complete Poems
Translated by Edmund Keeley and Philip Sherrard